Attention Games

Attention Games

101 Fun, Easy Games That Help Kids Learn to Focus

BARBARA SHER

ILLUSTRATIONS BY
RALPH BUTLER

JOSSEY-BASS
A Wiley Imprint
www.josseybass.com

Published by Jossey-Bass
A Wiley Imprint
989 Market Street, San Francisco, CA 94103-1741   www.josseybass.com

Jossey-Bass books and products are available through most bookstores. To contact Jossey-Bass
directly call our Customer Care Department within the U.S. at 800-956-7739, outside the U.S. at
317-572-3986, or fax 317-572-4002.

Jossey-Bass also publishes its books in a variety of electronic formats. Some content that appears in
print may not be available in electronic books.

Library of Congress Cataloging-in-Publication Data
Sher, Barbara.
  Attention games : 101 fun, easy games that help kids learn to focus / Barbara Sher ; illustration by
Ralph Butler.— 1st ed.
      p. cm.
  Includes index.
  ISBN-13: 978-0-471-73654-7 (alk. paper)
  ISBN-10: 0-471-73654-6 (alk. paper)
  1. Educational games. 2. Attention in children. I. Title: 101 fun, easy games that help kids learn to
focus. II. Title: One hundred and one fun, easy games that help kids learn to focus. III. Title.
  LB1029.G3S538 2006
  371.33'7—dc22

                              2006008090

Printed in the United States of America
FIRST EDITION

PB Printing   10 9 8 7 6 5 4 3 2

Acknowledgments - - - ~ - ~ - - ~ ~ - ~ -

To make a book, an author needs a publisher, editors, an artist, and a production crew. For this I have my very able editor, Kate Bradford; her competent assistant, Connie Santisteban; a creative illustrator, Ralph Butler; and a production crew headed up by the very capable Justin Frahm. I'm grateful for them all.

To come up with ideas for the text, an author needs inspirational coworkers and friends who are equally interested in the world of children. For this I have the "Dream Team" at the Special Education/Early Childhood Program in the Northern Mariana Islands of Saipan—namely, Dora Palacios-Won, Mark and Patty Staal, Jerry Diaz, Fidelia Ruben, Tracy Nance, Mercy Tisa, Ataur Rahman, Judy Hawkins, Yollanda Lelly, and Rita Olopai. I appreciate and adore them all.

To take pleasure in the writing process, an author needs loving support from friends and family. For this I have many wonderful people: Marissa and Mark SherKenney; Roxanne Sher-Skelton, Ehren Olson; Anna Sher; Fran Simon; Trisha and David Ferlic; Shirley Sher; Don Cohen; Monty Sher; Glo Harris; Bonnie, Jenna, Marc, Jacob, and Leslie Wilson; Maxwell, Griffin, Jessica, and Stewart Evans; Jenny Slack; Nolan and Manny Mariano; Rita Bonnici; Susan Book; Jill Derickson; Ericka Frink; and all my precious Humboldt County buddies. I love them all back.

But to make my book have heart, this author needed children to field test the games. My deep appreciation goes to all the children I play with every day in my work, especially the ones who show me that there really is something special about being "special." Thank you for teaching me that humans come in many flavors. And they are all good.

Contents

Introduction 1

How to Contact the Author 5

PART ONE Games for Infants 7

Follow My Face 9

Stick Out Your Tongue 11

The Glory of Hands 13

Sock on a Bottle 14

Perfect Rattles 15

First Exercises 17

Visually Amused 21

A Light Touch 22

Can You Hear What I Hear? 24

A Very Merry Unbirthday 26

Pokey Pudding Hole 27

Dangling Toys 28

Bat the Ball 31

High Chair Fling 32

Ice Cube on a Tray 34

If It Doesn't Hurt—It's a Toy 35

A Spotlight in the Dark 37

What's out There? 39

Where'd It Go? 41

PART TWO   **Games for 1- to 3-Year-Olds**   45

Bracelet of Leaves   47
The Enchantment of Water   48
Follow the Floating Feather   49
The Knocking Game   50
Ping-Pong Balls and Coffee Cans   51
Surprise Me   53
The Feely Game   54
What Is That Sound?   55
From Beginning to End   57
Being a Radio   59
Catch a Falling Scarf   60
Instant Picture   61
You've Got Mail   62
Kaleidoscope   63
Magnet Hunt   64
Put a Lid on It   66
Ooh—Smell This!   67
What's in the Sock?   69

PART THREE   **Games for 3- to 6-Year-Olds**   71

My Story Is the Best Story   73
Another Viewpoint   74
Art de Deux   76
Batting Practice   77
The Happening Book   78
Lessons from the Rocks   80
Mismatched Tea Party   81
Plenty Peanut Hunt   84
Regroup Time   85

Shadow Games   87
Deck of Cards   88
Hand on Top   89
How Many?   90
Indoor Picture Hunt   91
Mexican Yo-Yo   92
Mini-Montessori   94
Going on a Monster Hunt   97
Paint the World   99
The Perfect Gifts   100
Sounds Right   104
Word Matching   105

PART FOUR   Games for 6- to 12-Year-Olds   109

All the Things You Can Think Of   111
Back Writing   112
Belly Counts   113
Expanding Interest   114
Focused Fidgeting   116
Guess How Old   117
How Do You Look?   119
Junk Box Art   120
Name the Sounds   121
Navigator   122
Police Report   123
Ring of String   125
Shelf Paper Story   126
Thinking Box   127
I'm the Teacher   129
My Mind Is a TV Screen   130
Paper Plethora   132

Potato Puppets   133
Sensory Matching   135
Tile Painting   137
Backwards Time Management   138
Toe Stepping   140
Toothpick Art   141

PART FIVE   # Games for Teens   143

Accentuate the Positive   145
Achy Breaky Heart   146
Annoyed with the Flower Bud   147
Five Good Moments   149
Getting the Priorities   150
My Special Things   152
I'm Like That Sometimes   153
Imagine That!   155
Send Joy to Bulgaria   156
Life Is a Movie, and You Are the Star!   158
List Your Options   160
Name the Consequences   162
Postcard Diaries   164
Scriptwriter   165
Self-Portraits   166
Ten Breaths   167
The Home Videographer   169
Waiter, Take My Order   170
Flip-Flop Stamps   172
Word Puzzles   173

Index   175

Attention Games

Introduction

If you want to focus children's attention, you first have to capture their interest. In this book, I'll show you how to get children's attention with fun and interesting games and how to help them expand their powers of attention in ways that will benefit them throughout their lives.

Everyone is paying attention to something. What that something is and how long the attention is captured are the variables.

There are two forms of attention. One is open and global; you light on many different aspects of your surroundings for short periods of time. Open attention gives you an overall impression of your environment. Think of being at a party. You become aware of the general feel of the party by noticing people's body language as well as different sounds, smells, and sights. Your attention focuses on many things fleetingly to give you a holistic sense of what is happening. Or think of riding a bike. When you ride a bike, you can attend to steering, pedaling, and the traffic around you while also enjoying the feeling of the breeze blowing through your hair.

The second form of attention is more focused; you concentrate on one thing for long periods. Focused attention requires active filtering of excess information, and you notice details in sequences rather than all at once. Whereas global attention is like an overhead light, focused attention is like a flashlight with a narrow beam. This is the kind of attention required to do things like follow instructions, write an article, or do a crossword puzzle.

Everyone needs both of these types of attention. Open attention gives us a lot of information quickly and encourages creativity by causing us to notice connections and make new patterns. This creative trail helps us find new ways of seeing old things. At the same time, though, nothing can be accomplished without the absorbed, one-step-at-a-time perseverance of focused attention.

We do best when we are able to shift easily between an open state of awareness and a focused one.

Typical behavior for a child diagnosed with Attention Deficit Disorder (ADD) is to notice everything and filter nothing. Whereas another child may focus on the teacher, the child with ADD may instead notice the buzzing fly in the room, the birds fluttering in the trees outside the window, the whispering in the back of the room, the holes in the ceiling tile, and how the air from the vent is making a child's hair ribbons ripple. As one mother pointed out, "One thing about my kid—she sure is observant. She notices things no one else would notice, and she sees relationships between stuff out there that no one else would ever think of."

There is often a similar pattern in not being able to filter out the surrounding sounds or to resist going on a finger safari to reach out and touch all there is to touch.

And yet as Thomas Armstrong points out in his book *Myth of the ADD Child,* there is substantial evidence to suggest that children labeled ADD do not show distractibility in specific situations. One mother of a child diagnosed with ADD said, "My child is capable of long periods of concentration when he is watching his favorite sci-fi video or examining the inner workings of a pin-tumbler lock." It is also known that a child with attention difficulties can frequently focus well in a one-to-one situation with a caring adult and an activity that is of interest to the child.

As Dr. Mel Levine points out in his book *A Mind at a Time,* there's more that's right than wrong with these kids. Levine has seen children who suffer with weak attention control when young turn into remarkable adults. He comments, "I believe these children are challenging types of human variation rather than deviation. . . . What a crime to assume simply that all of these kids are damaged goods. After many years working with these individuals, I am impressed with how many of them turn out to be extraordinary adults. We just have to get them there."

Most of us use our own unique combination of open and focused attention. All of us would benefit from learning how to be better at one type or the other. This book is geared toward the "wellness model," which assumes that no person is broken and that everyone can gain from appropriate experiences. Being able to shift fluidly between open attention and focused concentration is a useful skill that everyone can learn and improve on.

Ideally we teach our children the skills of open and focused attention as infants, when they undergo the most rapid brain development. During this period, the child's brain is becoming "hard-wired," and she is particularly receptive to experiences. There are many games here to help the infant and toddler develop good attention skills from the start.

There are many games for preschool children that will encourage them to notice details in life. The more we notice the different aspects of a situation, the longer we will attend. Think about experiences you have had. For example, if someone points out to you a variety of wildflower, you are much more likely to pay attention to those flowers and even look for them the next time you go for a walk in the woods. Knowing about details in life increases your attention span.

There are many games in this book for school-age children that are novel to their routine experiences. Novelty raises a person's arousal level and therefore increases attentiveness. In order to learn, we all have to have a certain level of arousal. Too low, and we feel too sleepy to pay attention; too high, and we are too fidgety. It is thought that hyperactive children are actually trying to raise their arousal level because they have low interest in routines. Novelty sharpens their interest and helps them focus; their need for novelty explains why they do best in a school that emphasizes action-oriented, hands-on, project-based participation.

Playing these games can also raise children's self-esteem by showing children who have been labeled as lacking attention skills that they too have focusing abilities within them. And overabsorbed children whose attention is narrowly focused can learn the delights of opening their awareness to all that is.

As adolescents continue to develop their attentive skills, there is the added factor of increased anxiety because of the social desire to fit in. Games for these teenagers are geared toward reducing anxiety levels so they can be comfortable and better able to focus on the present moment.

The games and activities in this book are organized into those that encourage open attention, those that encourage focused attention skills, and those that encourage fluidity in shifting from one type of attention to the other.

The more we do anything, the better we get. And because enjoyable ways always make learning easier, all the games have one single important element in common—fun!

After interviewing a large number of teachers, Sandra Rief noted in her book *How to Reach and Teach ADD/ADHD Children,* "If these kids are happy and feel good about themselves, they will learn!"

Playing these games includes something else that is precious to children: *your* attention. Remember how it felt when you were a child and a loving adult took the time to play with you? It makes you feel that you matter. As an occupational therapist who has worked with all kinds of children for over thirty-five years, I see how children light up when they are given individual attention, and I know how good it feels to be the cause of that joy.

The games in this book benefit you both.

How to Contact the Author - - ~ - ~ - ~

Barbara has done workshops worldwide where participants learn by playing games and making games. In some workshops, participants make developmentally appropriate learning toys from "trash." In others, participants play games that use movement to teach academic skills or sensory-motor games to encourage integration. The emphasis is on fun games that children of different skill levels can play together.

And some workshops are done by participants playing a whole slew of games with their children with nothing fancier, for example, than newspapers.

She has taught teachers, therapists, parents, nurses, aides, students, and and other caregivers. Her workshops have been in orphanages, schools, hospitals, conferences and universities in Hong Kong, Vietnam, Cambodia, Laos, Fiji, Roratonga, New Zealand, Hawaii, Nicaragua, Honduras, Palau, Phonepei, Chuck, Kosrae, Saipan, Tinian, Rota and the United States.

If you are interested in her services as a consultant or a workshop leader or just want to talk about any of the games, email her at:

momsense@asis.com.

To see a description of her books, visit her website:

www. barbarashergames.com.

OTHER BOOKS/TAPES BY BARBARA SHER

Self-Esteem Games
Spirit Games
Smart Play
Extraordinary Games with Ordinary Things
Popular Games for Positive Play
Moving Right Along
28 Instant Song Games (CD and tape)

PART ONE

Games for Infants

The brain is not developed at birth. The heart has the same form from birth on, but the brain needs experiences to make pathways between the brain cells. We have one hundred billion brain cells at birth. The ones that aren't used die. We use them when we connect them, with synapses, to each other in meaningful ways.

By age three, one thousand billion connections have been created by repeating things over and over. Repetition creates patterns as one experience is connected to many similar experiences. In order to form these patterns, children need interaction.

The relationship between parent and child is crucial to brain development. Parents and caregivers have a marked affect on creating connections, because the pathways between brain cells are reinforced by what the infant sees, smells, hears, touches, and does during the first years of life. Children raised in deprived sensory environments where there is minimal touching, sounds, sights, and experience actually develop smaller brains. Experience literally grows brains. Even rats raised in cages full of toys have more brain mass than rats with no toys.

The games in this part of the book help form patterns by giving babies a rich sensory environment to attend to. There are many games that stimulate the infant's sensory systems of touch, sight, sound, and taste as well as games that give babies repeated experiences in mastering their motor skills. There are other games that encourage exploratory and dramatic play to help babies see connections in their daily environment.

All the games work on the principle of developing sustained attention by providing interesting age-appropriate experiences. The whole continuum of attention is stimulated, from narrow focusing, such as in the Ice Cube on a Tray activity, to global focusing, such as in the What's out There? activity.

Of course, each game also produces the important pleasurable feelings that come from just having a good time, and all the games are easy to do, requiring nothing more than what you'd find around the house.

It's easy to tell when babies are paying attention: their eyes widen; their bodies get very still. If they have enjoyed the experience before, their arms and legs will flail with excitement. When they have had enough stimulation, they will turn their heads and look away, maybe even making fussing sounds. You'll soon learn how to read your baby's cues so that you'll know when to give him both fun times and rest.

Follow My Face

There is nothing more interesting to infants than a human face. They are just programmed that way, and for a very good reason: survival. Making eye contact with an adult human on whom your survival depends increases the possibility of being noticed and cared for. Whose heart isn't tugged by the purposeful gaze of a newborn?

This is also one of the first experiences in focused attention that your newborn will have. Her instinct is to look at you. You expand that and increase her attention span by having her find your eyes again and again. The delightful part is that her attention is lovingly focused on you!

TYPE OF ATTENTION ENCOURAGED

Focused

MATERIALS

None

DIRECTIONS

Place your face close and directly in front of your infant's face. Babies are a bit nearsighted at first and see best at about the distance from the crook of a mother's cradling arm to her smiling face. Clever nature. Infants don't yet know how to distinguish what is foreground and what is background. Getting up close ensures that your baby can see you and that she notices you. Research has shown that babies are the most attentive when looking at a human face, so it shouldn't be hard to get her attention. Once you see that her eyes have widened and focused on you, give her praise, such as by saying, "Good, you see me!"

Now, slowly move your face so that it is at the side of her face. Softly call out her name until she moves her eyes and finds you again. Praise her some more: "You found me. Good for you!"

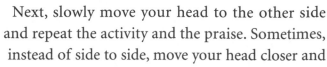

Next, slowly move your head to the other side and repeat the activity and the praise. Sometimes, instead of side to side, move your head closer and then farther away (near and far) or diagonally.

Continue the game until your child is tired of playing. You'll know when she is done by paying attention to her signals. If your infant is very still, it means she is attending and is interested in the game. If she turns her head away and starts to squirm, it means she's done for now.

Don't worry; she will love to play this again later, and you'll be helping her learn how to control the six muscles that control each eye and to coordinate the movements of both eyes together.

VARIATIONS

Here are some other ways to help your infant get a good eye workout and expand her ability to attend:

- Hang things above her bed that sway, such as wind chimes, scarves, and mobiles.
- Put a bird feeder outside her window.
- Reflect lights on the walls and ceiling of her darkened room.
- Place interesting designs or pictures on a nearby wall.

WHAT'S BEING LEARNED

A major lesson being learned, in addition to focusing, is developing eye control. Learning to control the muscles of the eyes, like any other muscle in the body, happens through practice. It is this control that will enable infants to scan their surroundings, notice different details, and thereby increase their awareness and intelligence.

Small movements of the eye also help the brain learn about space—for example, what is far, what is near, and what is on the side.

Cognitively, babies are also learning to distinguish what is the main figure and what is background.

Stick Out Your Tongue

One of the first ways I play with any infant is to stick out my tongue. It may make some parents wonder about me, but it never fails to fascinate the little one. Think about it. The tongue looks like some lively little snake coming out of your mouth.

I've done this game with infants as young as three months, and they always respond by thrusting out their own tongue in imitation, even if only the tip. Having control over the tongue's movement ensures that the infant will develop the ability to form different sounds and eventually words. Try it.

TYPE OF ATTENTION ENCOURAGED

Focused

MATERIALS

None

DIRECTIONS

Get your child's attention by softly calling to him and smiling. Once he notices you, stick out your tongue and waggle it a little. Tell him what you are doing: "It's my tongue." Tell him about his: "You have a tongue, too. Open your mouth. Let's see it," or words to that effect.

Keep wagging and maybe even add some soft sounds to keep his attention engaged. If you want, you can even gently touch his tongue to give him some sensory feedback on what part you are talking about.

Play the game as long as he is interested. Then do it another day, and once he gets it, add the variations.

VARIATIONS

Start showing him how to move his tongue in different directions. Start with side to side. Once he's got that movement, go to up-and-down movements. If you can curl your tongue, add that to his repertoire.

I also teach older babies this variation: I push my nose in, and my tongue pops out. I push my nose to one side, and my tongue goes to that side. When I push my nose to the other side, my tongue follows. I push my nose in again, and my tongue goes back into my mouth. I find little ones will stay very attentive and enjoy trying to imitate this.

WHAT'S BEING LEARNED

Babies are focusing their attention on a task that is within their motor ability. Because they are already nursing and suckling the breast or a bottle, they already tighten the muscles of their tongue to suck. This game makes babies aware of these muscles so that they can consciously control them.

Learning conscious control over isolated muscles is a vital skill. At first all babies flail their arms and legs about, but little by little they learn how to use one part of their body without moving any other part. They increase their internal awareness.

Playing this game with babies also shows them that you are a silly source of great fun and worth paying attention to!

The Glory of Hands

If you've been around babies before, you know there is that moment in their development, around the second to third month, when they discover their hands. They are so intrigued! They'll move them this way and that and experiment with opening and closing them and making their fingers flutter. Can you imagine how interesting that must be? Life is full!

You can help your child focus on her hands and begin this glorious discovery with something as simple as a "scrunchie." You'll also see how absorbed focusing can soothe the restlessness of a young baby.

TYPE OF ATTENTION ENCOURAGED

Focused

MATERIALS

Several scrunchies, which are ponytail holders made from colorful pieces of material of different sizes and various textures with elastic inside

DIRECTIONS

Place one scrunchie around the knuckles of her fingers, excluding the thumb. Experiment with finding or adjusting the scrunchie so that it is a comfortable fit for your baby's hand and is not too tight or too loose.

This game will increase her delight with her hands as you keep varying their appearance with scrunchies of differing colors and patterns.

Take the scrunchie off when your baby is not interested in it. If she starts to mouth it, it means she's discovered her hands and is starting to know how to use them. It's time for the next game!

VARIATIONS

◆ Put a scrunchie on her foot or ankle to help her notice her feet.

◆ Make a wrist or ankle bracelet by cutting elastic to just fit around your baby's wrist or ankle with a little overlap. Attach a bell that is too big to be swallowed (large jingle bells are especially easy to find and stock up on at Christmas, but handicraft stores have them year-round) and sew the ends of the elastic together.

◆ Instead of a bell, you can make and add a pom-pom that is too big to be swallowed. To make a pom-pom, cut a strip of heavy cardboard 1½ inches wide. Wrap a brightly colored yarn around it fifty times. Slip the yarn off the cardboard and tie it tightly around the middle with a piece of yarn about 9 inches long. Leave the ends of the 9-inch piece of yarn long for tying the pom-pom on to the elastic. Give the pom-pom a haircut by trimming off the longer pieces so that the fringe is even and fluffed out.

WHAT'S BEING LEARNED

Babies are beginning to master their body movements. In this game, babies are not only noticing their extremities but also learning to control their wrist, hand, finger, and foot movements as they move their hands and feet around to see the scrunchie from different angles or make the bell jingle.

As babies grow, with the right experiences, their dexterity will continue to improve and be a reliable source of attention.

Sock on a Bottle

When your baby is old enough to hold his own bottle, you can enrich that experience by creating a textural and visual delight with nothing more than a sock.

TYPE OF ATTENTION ENCOURAGED

Focused

MATERIALS

Variety of clean socks in different colors, patterns, and textures

DIRECTIONS

Place the bottom of your child's bottle into a clean sock that has a pleasing texture, color, or design. Hold the bottle in front of your baby, but wait until he focuses on the new element before giving it to him. Change to a different sock on another day to add the element of surprise and give a new experience.

VARIATION

Paint black dots or stripes on the bottle and encourage your baby to focus on the pattern for a moment by gently taking his hand in yours and touching the pattern together.

WHAT'S BEING LEARNED

This game strengthens tactile and visual skills. It also increases babies' awareness of the textures, patterns, and colors in their world. Their awareness will increase their interest in attending to these details as they grow.

Perfect Rattles

If you haven't switched over to digital photography or you're willing to go to a photo store and get its used film canisters, here's a quickie way to excite your child's attention: make interesting rattles that are just the right size for her hands.

TYPE OF ATTENTION ENCOURAGED

Focused

MATERIALS

4 or more clear film canisters (or any small clear container of a similar size, such as a cleaned pill bottle)

Small household items to put in canisters—for example, pennies, beans, salt, rice (can also be colored with food coloring), cornstarch, baking soda, buttons, and paper clips

Tape (optional)

DIRECTIONS

Put enough of any of the materials you've chosen in each film canister so that when it's shaken it makes a noise. Close tightly. (You might want to tape it closed if there is a toddler sibling who might open it and put the contents in her mouth.) Have some canisters contain all one material and others hold a mix of things.

Place one rattle in your baby's hand and place your hand over hers so that the rattle is still visible. Shake the rattle and either wait until she brings her hand to eye level or gently guide her hand with yours.

You can talk about what she is seeing: "Those are pennies. They make a loud sound" or "This is salt. It makes a soft sound."

The talking isn't intended to teach but merely to introduce new words and concepts.

Later, when your baby is lying on her belly, leave some of these rattles around to reach for and explore.

VARIATIONS

◆ Use small travel-size shampoo bottles or small clean and empty clear pill bottles, half-filled with colored water and objects that float, such as beads and sequins.

◆ Fill a toothpaste box with stones, sand, acorns, or similar material and cover it with contact paper. Children love to hear the sound of the objects sliding as they tip the box up and down.

WHAT'S BEING LEARNED

Babies are learning that they can cause things to happen, which is an important factor in getting and holding their attention. In this case, their attention is excited because shaking the rattle will cause a sound to happen and the items inside to move.

I can't stress enough the importance of giving children many different experiences and opportunities to explore. Understimulated children can be significantly delayed in their attention skills.

In this game, children are also learning about variations in sounds: some are loud, some are soft, and all have slightly different qualities. These differences further reward children's experience in attending.

When they are lying on their belly reaching and shaking the rattles, they have the added benefit of strengthening the muscles of their neck and back. This will later help them hold their head up so that they can look around and notice more things!

First Exercises

One of the first ways to help your baby learn to focus is to increase his awareness of his body and teach him how to make his body work. Infants are born with two arms and two legs, which they haven't a clue about how to work. They wave them around with great energy, but they need experience to learn how to make them do what they want. One of the largest tasks newborns are faced with is learning how to move their bodies and to isolate muscle groups for purposeful movement.

Imagine if you were to wake up one day with three extra appendages in a world where everyone has them and everyone but you uses them expertly. It will give you a sense of what infants have to accomplish.

You can help your infant gain this experience and in the process have loving, fun moments. Officially you'll be doing "range of motion" exercises in which you are giving your child the experience of moving his arms and legs in their full motoric range.

TYPE OF ATTENTION ENCOURAGED

Focused

MATERIALS

None

DIRECTIONS

When your child is lying on his back, place a hand on each of his arms. You can rub his arms first and talk about how beautiful they are and then sing or chant the song included here while moving his arms and then his legs in the movements described. Babies like rhythmic movements and a sure, firm touch. If a muscle feels tense, hold the limb by the elbow or knee joint and gently jiggle it to reduce tension. Repeat each section as often or as little as feels right for the moment.

I'm using the tune of "Frère Jacques" in this example. Feel free to use whatever tune you prefer or make up one of your own.

How do your arms move?
How do your arms move?
Up and down
Up and down
Feel your arms go up now
Feel your arms go down now
Up and down
Up and down

How else do your arms move?
How else do your arms move?
In and out (or open and close)
In and out
Feel your arms go in now
Feel your arms go out now
In and out
In and out

How do you legs move?
How do your legs move?
Up and down
Up and down

Feel your legs go up now
Feel your legs go down now
Up and down
Up and down

How else do your legs move?
How else do your legs move?
In and out (or open and close)
In and out
Feel your legs go in now
Feel your legs go out now
In and out
In and out

VARIATIONS

◆ You can do this with other body movements:

Arms bend and straighten

Arms rotate (hold the elbow joint and bring the palms up and then down)

Legs bend and straighten

Legs rotate (hold on to the knee and gently make the foot go from side to side)

Hips go side to side when legs are bent

Feet and hands go up and down and make circles

◆ You can also vary the speed of the movements by changing the tune. Singing to the tune of "Tea for Two," for example, can make for a different rhythm:

> Up and down and up and down
> And in and out and in and out
> And back and forth and back and forth
> We dooooooooo to—ge——ther

◆ You can give your child time to experiment with movements by providing a large, safe, flat space on which he might roll around and try out different ways of moving. It's nice for babies if some time is spent without diapers and other restricting clothes.

◆ Putting bells on booties or wrists (or both) rewards your newborn's efforts with a lovely tinkle.

WHAT'S BEING LEARNED

Bringing a focused awareness to the body starts babies on the path to coordination and gracefulness.

Continued mastery over the body helps children become more willing to pay attention to what their body is doing. The body will be a source of expected satisfaction and not clumsy frustration.

Visually Amused

It can be boring to be an infant, especially if the child spends a lot of time on her back looking at nothing. No wonder babies can look "spaced out," with vacant sleepy eyes. At this stage, the only way babies can entertain themselves is by watching things. You can begin to show your infant the joys of focusing by dangling a variety of interesting things to watch.

Because anything gets boring after a while, notice when your newborn no longer seems interested and change the objects. Listed here are some easy things to put on a hanger that will provide a visually amusing variety and will be easy for you to do.

TYPE OF ATTENTION ENCOURAGED

Open

MATERIALS

Coat hanger

Things to hang from the hanger—for example, ribbons, scarves, foil tart pans, colorful yarn, strips of fabric, wind chimes, bells, Christmas ornaments, chains of paper clips, strips of aluminum foil, pieces of pretty wrapping paper, feathers, flowers, necklaces, beads, leaves, spoons, cloth strips cut with pinking shears, and so on

DIRECTIONS

Make a hanger with some fascinating things hanging from it. Make sure, of course, that everything is tied on well. Tie a piece of string to the hanger and tie the other end over the changing table or above where your baby sleeps, sits in a baby seat, or lies on the floor. I find a cup hook works well for holding the hanger. The objects on the hanger should be close enough for your baby to see (7 to 24 inches away) but *out of reach.*

If you place the hanger near an open window or gently blowing fan, you add movement. Babies are fascinated by things that move.

VARIATIONS

- Hang dry flowers from an old umbrella frame.
- Hang a hula hoop and tie ribbons to it.
- Place a small fish bowl or aquarium so that your baby can easily see it from her bed or seat.

WHAT'S BEING LEARNED

Babies are beginning to distinguish foreground from background. Their first visual awareness is a blur of color and motion out of which details begin to emerge.

Babies are also learning that their world has many fascinating things in it, and a fascinated, focused infant is a happy, pleasant one.

A Light Touch

The ability to lovingly touch others starts when an infant is first lovingly touched. In those first few months when he is learning if this is a safe and friendly world, it's extremely important that he be tenderly held, cuddled, rocked, and caressed.

Touching also gives your baby feedback about his body parts. Touching ever so lightly encourages him to pay even closer attention to what is happening to his body.

TYPE OF ATTENTION ENCOURAGED

Focused

MATERIALS

Feather or paintbrush

DIRECTIONS

Stroke your baby's different body parts with the feather or paintbrush and name the body part being touched—for example, "I'm touching your leg. Do you feel it? I'm stroking your sweet little leg. Now I'm touching your arm."

VARIATIONS

◆ Touch your baby in a variety of ways, such as with gentle squeezing, massaging, patting, and rubbing.

◆ Give him experience with different types of textures. Rub your baby's body with materials of different textures, such as silk, velvet, wool, cotton ball, corduroy, and powder puffs. Talk about the differences with your darling: "Isn't this velvet soft. It's so soft. Feel this corduroy. It's a bit rougher, isn't it?"

◆ Make or buy a quilt that has a variety of textures for the baby to lie on.

◆ Pat the soles of your baby's feet to stimulate muscles, encourage strong bones, and increase his awareness of the part he'll later need to control for walking.

◆ Put applesauce on your baby's clean foot so that he can lick it off and stimulate his foot muscles.

◆ When putting your baby to bed, pat different parts of his body and say "Good night toes," "Good night legs," and so on.

◆ And I guess it's not news that babies love to have their bodies kissed, especially their bellies!

WHAT'S BEING LEARNED

Rubbing, stroking, massaging, holding, patting, and other tactile experiences stimulate the central nervous system. Touch activates the nerves in the muscles and joints, which causes children to be aware of what is going on in their body. This internal focusing gives babies a head start on controlling their own musculature, which leads to better coordination. When children have confidence in their coordination, they are much more willing to pay attention when playing sports, dancing, hiking, and doing other physical things.

Can You Hear What I Hear?

You can help your child learn that sound coming into one ear means that the source of the sound is coming from that side, and sound coming equally into both ears means that the source of the sound is either above, below, or in front of her. Although this may seem obvious, the reality is that, like everything else, this is something we all have to learn from experience. You can help reinforce your child's learning by playing this game.

TYPE OF ATTENTION ENCOURAGED

Focused
(Variations are open and focused)

MATERIALS

Rattle
Music

DIRECTIONS

While your baby is lying on her back, shake a rattle on one side of her head and out of sight of her eyes. When she turns her head to find the source of the noise, praise her skill. "You found the rattle, you smart girl, you!" Keep moving the rattle around in different locations, including above and below her, while encouraging your infant to find the sound. "Where is it now? Can you find it? You did!" Change the noisemaker to keep the game interesting.

VARIATIONS

You can also help your child develop the ability to hear a wide range of sounds and acquire an ear for music by introducing a variety of pleasant sounds. Here are some ideas:

◆ Sing words sometimes instead of speaking them.

◆ Make music for your baby even if it is only off-key crooning to the rhythm of a spoon on a pan. It's nice to learn we can make our own music.

◆ Play her a variety of music, such as jazz, classical, swing, and rock and roll. Keep a nice balance between music and silence so that your baby can develop a sensitive ear. (Sound that is on all the time gets "tuned out," and the child begins to use her hearing less.)

◆ Hang a pair of noisemaking items, such as two spoons, above where she lies down so that she can swat at them to make a sound.

◆ Speak in different pitches to your baby. Sometimes talk in a whisper; other times modulate between loud and soft. Sometimes hum or whistle.

◆ Hang wind chimes outside her window. There are a variety of kinds you can get. The ones made of bamboo are quite different from the ones made of steel pipes. The ones made from shells tinkle differently than the ones made of glass.

◆ Place a ticking clock near where your child naps. Perhaps it will remind her of the time she lay close to her mother's heart.

WHAT'S BEING LEARNED

Besides learning how to tell the location of sound, babies are learning the delights of listening, especially with all the variations. Listening requires a shift in consciousness to make it an active skill, a changing of gears. As adults, we know the difference between hearing people talk and really listening to what they are saying, or hearing music in the background and really listening to it. This awareness is what is being developed and encouraged here.

A Very Merry Unbirthday

Sometime when you happen to pass a party store or a party decoration section, grab a few items. You can use them at unexpected times to delight your child's senses.

TYPE OF ATTENTION ENCOURAGED

Open

MATERIALS

Party decorations, such as crepe-paper streamers, paper flower garlands, kites, and balloons

DIRECTIONS

Hang streamers and colorful balloons or whatever else appeals to you, such as kites or Mexican paper flower garlands, in the room while your baby is sleeping.

When he wakes up and after he has become adjusted to being awake, let him discover the new decorations for himself or hold him up to see them. Get the thrill of watching the delight and surprise on your baby's face when he notices the unexpected visual fiesta.

If you know the words to the unbirthday song from *Alice in Wonderland,* here's your opportunity to sing it! It starts off like this:

> A very merry unbirthday to you—to you
>
> A very merry unbirthday to me—to me

VARIATION

Place an unexpected new item in a place where your baby is sure to notice, such as above the changing table or across from his car seat.

WHAT'S BEING LEARNED

When babies are rewarded for looking around and seeing something unexpected and interesting, they develop the habit of scanning their environment to look for the familiar and the new. This encourages their ability to attend to details in their environment. This scanning also helps develop their control over eye muscles and increases their ability to focus their eyes to see farther distances, which extends the number of things to notice.

Pokey Pudding Hole

Infants' fingers go from chubby little things to precise instruments that can start picking lint off the floor and later type on keyboards. The first step in digit development is isolating the index finger. Babies who point have learned to do that. You can help your little one learn that first important trick in a most delicious way using the Pokey Pudding Hole.

TYPE OF ATTENTION ENCOURAGED

Focused

MATERIALS

Small packaged pudding or yogurt cup
Knife

DIRECTIONS

Buy a small pudding or yogurt cup in the refrigerated section of the grocery store. Remove the plastic lid and cut the foil lining of the container so that there is a small hole just a little bit bigger than the size of the baby's index finger. Make sure the edge of the hole is smooth to the touch.

Let your baby experiment with poking her finger in the hole. Because curious babies check out everything they touch by putting it in their mouths, your child won't need much encouragement to taste the pudding or yogurt and suck it off her finger.

VARIATIONS

When the yogurt is no longer usable and she's done with that game, wash out the container and put different things inside for her to poke and explore: cotton balls, soft cloth in different textures, and so on. (You might need to retape the foil lining.) Any substance that isn't harmful and will stimulate her curiosity will work.

WHAT'S BEING LEARNED

By learning how to isolate their index finger, babies are learning the first step in controlling the muscles of their fingers. This skill begins a lifetime of concentrating on all the wonderful things that competent hands can do. If you know you can rely on your hands to do what you want, then you are more likely to concentrate on a task. Avoiding frustration is one of the reasons children move on to something else. Helping our children be dexterous is something we can do.

Dangling Toys

There comes a time for babies, usually around eight to twelve weeks of age, when looking without touching becomes boring. Now he will not only look intently at a dangling toy but also take a swipe at it. Contact may be by chance at first, but with practice, he'll go from swiping to grabbing to pulling.

Keep your child's attention level high by providing things worth reaching for. And you're not stuck with only plastic cartoon toys. You can use whatever is in the house or buy inexpensive things that provide tactile and sound input.

TYPES OF ATTENTION ENCOURAGED

Open and focused

MATERIALS

Bungee cord, tie, or belt

Elastic, string, or plastic shower curtain rings

Household items to hang—for example:

> Stuffed sock
>
> Bag of marbles in very secure bag
>
> Measuring spoons
>
> Film canisters
>
> Empty spools of thread strung together
>
> Plastic Easter eggs filled and taped
>
> Aluminum pie plates facing each other and taped securely together with noisy things, such as shells or beans, inside
>
> Stuffed wool or cotton glove
>
> Soft cloth in different colors
>
> Ribbons
>
> Sponges
>
> Napkin rings
>
> Heavy ply or doubled surgical gloves with different things in the fingers, such as rice, flour, cornstarch, and beans
>
> Small zip-type freezer bag with squishy stuff inside, such as pudding or peanut butter
>
> Stuffed nylon hose with bells inside

DIRECTIONS

Hang toys from a commercial baby arch or from a bungee cord, a tie, or a belt strung between two legs of a table. Use either elastic, string, or shower rings linked together to hang the toys. Be sure the toys are hanging low enough so that a child sitting on the floor, in an infant seat, or lying on his back can easily reach them. And be sure the main cord is high enough that your baby can't get tangled in it.

VARIATION

Hang one string longer than the rest and add a plastic bracelet or shower ring to the end of that string so that when your baby pulls it, everything rattles and shakes and makes noise at once.

WHAT'S BEING LEARNED

Babies are learning to scan a collection of objects and then pick one to consciously swat at or grasp. All their attention is engaged as they practice finding the exact muscles and power needed to accomplish the task.

If you put the objects on elastic, your little one is also building arm strength because the items will require more tugging.

Bat the Ball

Batting a ball can keep a baby fascinated for long periods. There's the thrill of connecting with a ball and making it move and the amazing sight of seeing it come back again.

TYPE OF ATTENTION ENCOURAGED

Focused

MATERIALS

Tennis ball
String
Knife

DIRECTIONS

Using a sharp knife, make a small slit (about ¾-inch wide) in a tennis ball. Tie several knots in the end of the string and poke the knotted end into the slit. The knots will prevent the string from slipping out.

If you have a little bell available, slip that into the slit too.

Tie the other end of the string to a kitchen drawer handle. Pull the drawer out a few inches so that when your baby is sitting on the floor or in an infant seat, she can bat it back and forth like a tetherball. The ball should hang a bit above her head so that it won't swing into her face.

Make sure that if she pulls downward on the ball, the drawer won't fall and nothing will fall out. You'll want to keep an eye on your baby as she does this activity to be sure her hand doesn't tangle in the string. You might even want to have a turn batting it yourself!

VARIATION

Tie the end of the string to a tray of a high chair so that she can throw the ball and pull the string to get the ball back.

WHAT'S BEING LEARNED

Babies are learning eye-hand coordination and are developing their arm muscles. They are also developing binocular depth perception and increasing control over their eye muscles.

The challenge of connecting with the ball enhances babies' ability to stay focused for long periods.

High Chair Fling

Babies love to throw things, especially from the height of their high chair. This is a great way for children to learn how to open their hands. Flexing their fingers to grab is a reflex that comes with birth. Anyone who has had an infant grab his or her hair knows they are great at grasping and not so great at releasing. Babies need to learn how to release that grasp by extending the finger muscles. Throwing things is one of the ways they have fun learning it.

It's also one of the ways you may get more exercise than you might want by continually having to bend down to pick up the thrown items.

Reduce your end of the job without depriving your baby of the thrill of flinging by tying different household items to one end of a short string and the other end to the high chair.

TYPE OF ATTENTION ENCOURAGED

Focused

MATERIALS

String or yarn

Household items to tie on—for example:

> Sponge
>
> Small boxes, such as jewelry
> boxes
>
> Wiffle balls
>
> Net bag with cotton inside
>
> Aluminum foil balls
>
> Feathers
>
> Stuffed animals

DIRECTIONS

Collect a few different items that will all feel different when thrown. For example, flinging a feather will feel different than flinging a Wiffle ball. Tie one end of a string to the item and tie the other to the high chair. You probably won't have to demonstrate the flinging part. Babies do that naturally! The possibly new and interesting part for him will be pulling the string and getting the toy back.

VARIATION

Instead of tying the string, you can tape the end of the string to the high chair leg or tray table with duct tape. Of course, if the tape is within reach, your baby will probably get interested in picking at the tape and loosening it. Make sure the piece is too big to swallow if he is successful.

WHAT'S BEING LEARNED

Babies are receiving feedback from their muscles that some items take more effort to throw than others, and they are learning to focus on this internal sensation. Later they will use this information in many ways, such as in judging how hard to throw a ball to hit a target or how hard to press a pencil so the point doesn't break.

Ice Cube on a Tray

Having a lot of interesting things to focus on in the short term sets a baby up with the expectation that life has many things to notice. In this game, a simple ice cube tossed on a high chair tray can provide some focused fun as it skitters to-and-fro and your baby tries to catch it.

When my children were babies, I noticed that they always got fussy just about the time I was making dinner. I think it was the smells that reminded them they were getting hungry. Give them something immediate to focus on, and make both of your lives easier!

TYPE OF ATTENTION ENCOURAGED

Focused

MATERIALS

Ice cubes
Food coloring (optional)

DIRECTIONS

Place a large ice cube on your child's tray. (For added interest, make colored ice cubes using the food coloring.) She'll probably catch it and suck on it for a while, then lose it again and chase it around some more. Keep an eye out that it hasn't melted so much that it might be small enough to swallow. Before you take the small cube away, replace it with another large one.

Your baby will also enjoy splashing the melted water.

VARIATIONS

◆ You could also make the ice cubes out of juice.

◆ If you don't mind messy, here are other interesting things to place on your baby's tray to capture her attention:

Soy sauce, mild mustard, or ketchup to squiggle around with her fingers

Whipped cream or meringue to poke and lick

Cornstarch on a secured mirror to see her reflection come in and out of focus

Jell-O blocks to touch and to watch shimmy and shake

WHAT'S BEING LEARNED

In terms of physical development, babies are practicing their eye-hand coordination. They have to keep an eye on the moving object and coordinate their hands in just the right place to catch the slippery thing. This task requires total concentration and extends their ability to pay attention.

If It Doesn't Hurt—It's a Toy

Children are very curious about all the things around them, especially if they see that these objects interest you. It's getting more common these days to find a very young child who can't even walk who already knows how to use the remote control for the television!

There are thousands of things that are acceptable for babies to explore. To encourage this innate instinct of exploration, keep out of reach the things that your baby can't explore, then just let him loose on his own to find the things that make up his world. You can also provide new things to examine.

Once they have looked at an object from every angle and discovered how it smells and tastes, babies are usually bored with it and try new ways of dealing

with it, like throwing it out the window and watching it bounce. Change the objects, and you'll renew your baby's interest. Anyone who has had to distract a fussy child knows well the effectiveness of searching in a purse, pocket, or drawer to find something new for your baby to examine.

TYPES OF ATTENTION ENCOURAGED

Open and focused

MATERIALS

My motto in selecting the right kind of item is simple: if it isn't going to hurt, it's a toy. That means the object has to have no sharp edges; it must be too large to swallow; it cannot be harmful if put in the mouth; and it must have nothing that can pinch or harm in any way.

A few interesting toys you can find around the house that you may not have thought of are listed here:

Tea infuser	Melon ball maker
Funnel	Plastic cookie cutter
Small strainer	Bottle stopper
Roll of masking tape	Nail brush
Pieces of junk mail	Napkin rings
Rubber glove	Bendable straws
Pastry brush	Measuring cups
Whistle	Measuring spoons
Empty plastic squeeze bottles	Flashlights
Sturdy plastic bracelets	Pleated hand fan
Tape	Rolls of cloth
Empty water bottles	Cassette tape box
Bandage box with flip-up lid	Desk organizer
Film canisters	Mailing tubes
Old deck of cards	Cardboard juice cans and lids
Empty plastic cosmetic jars and travel-size bottles	

DIRECTIONS

Gather a few items and keep them in a small box, such as a tackle box or shoe box. Let your child rifle through them. Change them according to your child's interest level. Keep an eye out for intriguing stuff at garage sales and secondhand stores.

VARIATIONS

Almost endless!

WHAT'S BEING LEARNED

Exposure to many items will encourage children's innate curiosity, a quality that will serve them well in school and in life. Sometimes curiosity is stifled at an early age by parents who overprotect their child by not permitting him to satisfy his natural instinct to explore.

Besides focusing in on the details of the different items, children are developing an open awareness of several different things at once. They are making new connections and seeing patterns: "Hmmm, all these things have empty insides, and you can put stuff into them. And if you turn them over, things fall out! But with this one, it only comes out if you turn it a certain way . . . hmmm."

This kind of experimentation encourages children to pay attention for longer periods because interesting differences and similarities appear.

A Spotlight in the Dark

Babies are fascinated with anything new. It's fun for us to be with a little one when she discovers something for the first time. In this game it's the delight of a flashlight in the dark.

TYPES OF ATTENTION ENCOURAGED

Open and focused

MATERIALS

One or two flashlights

DIRECTIONS

Keep the lights off in the room you are in and scan the room with a flashlight, spotlighting different familiar things. "Look—there's the television. Here is the table, and there is your high chair."

VARIATIONS

You know your little one is going to want a chance to hold the flashlight. Let her. She can shine it wherever she wants, or ask her to find, by pointing with her flashlight, an object you name.

As she gets older and more coordinated, continue this game, but now you both have flashlights; encourage her to "catch" your spotlight by covering your spotlight with hers. Then it's your turn to chase next.

WHAT'S BEING LEARNED

Spotlighting singles out individual objects on which to focus; scanning the room to find different objects promotes open awareness.

This game also reinforces the knowledge that things that can't be seen still exist. Even though one can't see the chair in the dark, for example, it is still there. Watch where you walk!

Following the light with their eyes also helps babies' developing visual system.

What's out There?

On the Mr. Roger's Neighborhood *television program, he had a segment called "These are the people in your neighborhood," because he knew that children are curious about what is around them.*

Even infants are curious about what's around them, and often a fussy baby will quiet down when taken to see What's out There.

Stimulate your baby's interest in his environment from the very start by taking a tour of his world, both inside and out.

TYPE OF ATTENTION ENCOURAGED

Open

MATERIALS

None

DIRECTIONS

Hold your baby so that he has a good view of the world by looking over your shoulder or facing forward. Take a tour of your home, yard, and

neighborhood. Walk up close to various things so that your baby has a near view and talk about what you are looking at.

"This is a photo of your grandfather. We took it on a fishing trip up North. He was so proud of that fish!"

"This is where we keep food so it stays cold."

"This is the biggest tree in our yard. Look how the green leaves are turning red. I love this time of year."

"This is a golden daffodil. I feel happy just looking at it."

"This is the store where we buy our groceries."

Your infant, of course, won't understand a word you're saying, but he will get the sense that things have words attached to them and will be fascinated with all that is out there.

He will also feel the pleasure in your voice and enjoy the conversational tone. Later, because of this experience and others like them, he will develop his own ability to converse pleasantly.

Be alert to when your baby starts to look away or fusses; he's letting you know he has had enough stimulation for the moment and needs quiet. Do it again another day.

VARIATIONS

This is a game whose variations continue throughout your baby's childhood. You can keep showing your child new things until the time comes when he starts showing *you* what's new!

WHAT'S BEING LEARNED

♦ Babies are developing their eyesight and visual acuity.

♦ They are increasing their ability to focus on things that are close and things that are distant.

- ◆ They are developing their perceptual knowledge of the many things there are to see, feel, and smell.

- ◆ They are developing their color vision, which comes in when they are around two to three months of age.

- ◆ They are being introduced to the idea that there are many things in their neighborhood and that these things have names.

- ◆ They are feeling that the world is a safe place to be because they are experiencing it from the loving safety of their parent's or loved one's arms.

- ◆ They are increasing their ability to pay attention by realizing that there are many things worth attending to in their life.

All this, thanks to you.

Where'd It Go?

Babies love hide-and-seek games. You've probably already had the fun of playing peek-a-boo with your child and watching her delight when your face reappears. Peek-a-boo is the first hide-and-seek game. In this game of Where'd It Go? you increase the challenge as your baby gets more adept.

TYPES OF ATTENTION ENCOURAGED

Open and focused

MATERIALS

Scarf

Box

Bag

Toy or other small object for hiding

DIRECTIONS

There is a progression to the challenge of finding hidden objects. Start with the easiest and over time progress to the most difficult.

1. Hide something from your baby under a scarf while she is watching and ask her "Where did the _____ go?"

2. Hide something behind an object, such as a box, when your baby is not watching. Leave a bit of the object showing and ask her to find it.

3. Hide the object behind the box with nothing showing and ask her to look for it.

4. Hide something inside a paper bag that's in her immediate vicinity.

5. Hide something behind the box *and* under a scarf before you make your request.

6. Hide something behind the box *and* under the scarf *and* inside the paper bag

VARIATIONS

♦ Get a yogurt container and a Popsicle stick. Draw a face on one end of the stick or paste on a face. Make a hole in the bottom of the yogurt container and push the stick through it. In front of your child, push the stick up and down so that the face appears over the rim of the container and then disappears. "Where'd it go?" "There it is!" (This is an activity you do. Be cautious about letting your baby have the stick.)

♦ Paste a small picture in an empty matchbox, small jewelry box, metal bandage box, or any box with a flip-up lid. Show an older baby (around one year old) how to open it to make the picture appear and close it to make it disappear.

♦ Get a mailing tube or the tube from a paper towel roll. Place a small car on one end and tilt the tube so that the car reappears on the other end. Let your baby experiment with putting the car in the tube and tilting it.

WHAT'S BEING LEARNED

Babies are learning that things they can't see still exist. It is this sense of "object permanence" that helps babies not cry when their mother is out of sight. Babies come to learn that even though their parent is gone, she still exists and they are still safe.

Babies also have to scan their environment for the missing item and then zero in on where it is, which reinforces both open and focused attention.

- - ˅ - ˅ - ˅ -

PART TWO

Games for 1- to 3-Year-Olds

Toddlers are learning about their world at a rapid pace. They are refining their sensory awareness so that they can interpret and anticipate what their senses are telling them, and increasing their motor skills so that they can use their bodies to achieve desired goals.

Both these skills require the ability to pay attention to what is happening around them and what is happening inside them. The games in this part of the book are designed to give children experience in these areas so that they can expand their ability to be attentive to everything going on around and within them.

Bracelet of Leaves

You can encourage your little one to notice the many shapes of leaves by making a masking tape leaf bracelet. It will give a focus to your child's outdoor time and increase his ability to scan and explore.

TYPES OF ATTENTION ENCOURAGED

Open and focused

MATERIALS

Masking tape
Leaves

DIRECTIONS

Wrap a piece of masking tape around your child's wrist, sticky side up, and then go exploring to find wonderful leaves and other interesting things to attach to the bracelet.

Before bedtime, snip the bracelet off and attach it next to his bed or somewhere in view so he can have a visual reminder of that fun experience.

VARIATIONS

◆ Make a flower bracelet. Collect little wildflowers.

◆ Wrap tape around the sleeves of your child's coat so that larger leaves or flowers can be included.

WHAT'S BEING LEARNED

Children are scanning the environment to find the leaves needed to enhance their bracelet. Then, with help, they are noticing the different details of the various leaves, such as color patterns, shape, and vein configuration. "Look how this leaf is shaped like a heart and this one looks more like an arrow."

This game will help make them generally more attentive to their environment on other days.

The Enchantment of Water

Although the "equipment" may seem too simple, a sponge and a bowl of water can provide some interesting focusing times for your toddler. (CAUTION: never leave a child alone near even very shallow water.)

TYPE OF ATTENTION ENCOURAGED

Focused

MATERIALS

Large dish pan or bowl
Clean, dry sponges

DIRECTIONS

Cut the sponges into pieces that your child's hand can easily squeeze but that are too big to swallow.

In a place you don't mind getting wet, have your child sit in front of a large dish pan. Put a shallow amount of water in the pan and toss in the sponges. Let your child have the fun of seeing the sponges float when dry and then noticing what happens as they get wet. Show your child how to soak up the water with the sponge and then squeeze it out.

VARIATIONS

♦ Cut a plastic bottle in half so that the top half is a funnel and the bottom is a cup. Tape the edges with duct tape to cover up any sharp edges. Make the cup more interesting by punching holes in the sides so that when it's full, water sprinkles out of the sides. Show your child how to squeeze water from the sponge into the funnel or the cup and watch what happens to the water.

♦ Put a tennis ball in the water so that your child can chase it around with her hand as it moves freely in the dish pan.

♦ Add corks to the water and teach your little one to blow through a straw and make the corks move about.

♦ Add large chunks of ice by freezing water inside an empty milk carton. Add food coloring and even small toys to the water before freezing, if you want.

♦ These same games can be played in the bath or a toddler pool.

WHAT'S BEING LEARNED

Children are getting their first lesson in the magic of things changing properties when they get wet. In this case, they are observing something that floats when it's dry and sinks when it's wet.

Children also have the opportunity to be captivated by the behavior of water, such as how it can pour through and out of different types of containers.

These are experiences that will absorb children's interest and show them that there are fascinating things in their world to explore.

Follow the Floating Feather

As mesmerizing as watching dancing dust motes, following the trajectory of a feather is both compelling and calming.

My friend Jenny discovered this game when dropping a feather for her son to watch. He was so fascinated by the feather's moving with the air currents as it gently floated down that he wanted to keep repeating the game.

I've even used the fascination with feather movements with a group of older children. They were wild and winding down from playing a series of lively movement games. I could feel that the teacher was a little worried about the high energy. I ended the session by standing them in a circle and having them gently blow a feather from one person to the next. Peace and calm prevailed.

TYPE OF ATTENTION ENCOURAGED

Focused

MATERIALS

One or more feathers. (A single feather will do, but you can buy a whole bag of multicolored feathers at a craft store.)

DIRECTIONS

Drop the feather and encourage your child to watch it as it slowly drops. To help him keep his eye on the feather's movement, suggest that he catch it as it falls.

Drop the feather from different heights or in different places in the room or outside to help him notice how movement is affected by air currents.

VARIATION

Blow the feather to your child and ask him to blow it back to you.

WHAT'S BEING LEARNED

In addition to increasing children's focusing skills, watching the movement of the feather enhances the control, strength, and flexibility of their eye muscles.

By noticing the differences in how the feather behaves in different air currents, children are becoming aware of the subtle effects of air movement. You can enlarge on this awareness by pointing out the different directions that leaves flutter and flower stalks bend when affected by the wind.

The Knocking Game

Listening to and identifying the different sounds objects make when you knock on them is a game that can be played at any time. This makes it an ideal game to play to help little ones let go of their fussing and change their focus.

TYPES OF ATTENTION ENCOURAGED

Open and focused

MATERIALS

Common objects found around the house
Spoon (optional)

DIRECTIONS

Ask your player to close her eyes and turn her back to you. Then see if she can guess the object you are knocking on with your fist. Start with easy things, such as a table and a window, and work toward sounds that are harder to identify, such as knocking on a book or lamp.

Take a turn being the identifier and let your child scan the room and be the knocker.

VARIATION

Use a spoon instead of your fist to knock on things.

WHAT'S BEING LEARNED

Children are learning to listen carefully and pay attention to differences in sounds.

Their vocabulary is also increased as you introduce new words to describe sounds, such as *chiming, tinny, hollow,* or *muffled.*

Ping-Pong Balls and Coffee Cans

There is something about Ping-Pong balls that is delightful to a child. Maybe it's that they are just the right size and weight for small fingers. Maybe it's because they make such a pleasant syncopated tapping sound when they bounce on the floor. Or maybe it's that they bounce in unpredictable patterns that are interesting to the eye.

The title of this game, Ping-Pong Balls and Coffee Cans, is all that probably needs to be said in explanation. The sound of a Ping-Pong ball falling into an empty coffee can and the challenge of getting one in will keep your one- to two-year-old delighted, involved, and attentive.

TYPE OF ATTENTION ENCOURAGED

Focused

MATERIALS

Empty coffee can

5 or more Ping-Pong balls

DIRECTIONS

Have your child stand on the floor with a coffee can at his feet. Give him a small basket or other container of Ping-Pong balls and show him how to drop them, one by one, into the can.

VARIATIONS

◆ As his aim increases in accuracy, raise the challenge by having him stand on a sturdy stool or chair.

◆ Place the can at varying distances away and take turns with your child trying to get the ball in the can.

◆ Ping-Pong balls will be bouncing all over the place, but that's a good thing. You can encourage your child to try out different ways to play with these delightful little balls, such as by using one ball to hit another.

WHAT'S BEING LEARNED

Children are focusing on making the Ping-Pong balls go in the can and developing their eye-hand coordination. They are also taking in the sensory details of the game, learning about weight, movement, size, shape, and sound.

If they make up their own variations of the game, their creativity is also being stimulated.

- ˋ ˇ ˋ ˇ ˋ ˇ ˋ ˇ ˋ ˇ ˋ ˇ ˋ ˇ ˋ ˇ ˋ ˇ ˋ ˋ

Surprise Me

Expecting the unexpected keeps young children interested and focused on their surroundings and the people in it. This is a simple game that you probably do anyway, with one little twist.

TYPE OF ATTENTION ENCOURAGED

Open

MATERIALS

Small items found around the house, such as corks, coins, pen tops, and marbles. (CAUTION: to avoid the possibility that your child might put these objects in her mouth, be sure not to let her have any of them.)

DIRECTIONS

Hide something, such as a cork, in your fist and let your little one pry open your fingers one at a time to find the treasure. Switch the object to the other hand. Let her open your fingers to find it again.

Now comes the SURPRISE part. After playing the game several times, surreptitiously slip a coin or other small object into your fist instead of the cork. The next uncurling of your fingers will surprise and delight your child. Expect her to want you to do it again many times. When she least expects it, changes the item again!

VARIATIONS

You could hide things under one of three upside-down cans. You scoot the cans around, and your player has to point to the can that has the hidden object under it. If you are very quick or can distract her attention for a moment ("Hey, look at that bird. Oh, you must have missed it"), switch the object under the can and surprise her.

WHAT'S BEING LEARNED

Showing children that at any point, things may be delightfully different than they expected gives them a lifelong gift. It is this expectation that keeps us keen and pleasantly alert to life's possible surprises.

The Feely Game

Babies first get information about objects by putting them on their lips and into their mouths, the most sensitive areas of their body. Later, they learn to use their fingertips for this information and begin to get pleasure from the simple act of stroking the surfaces of things. This stroking stimulates the nerve receptors in their skin, which helps them learn to distinguish differences in textures.

In this game, you encourage that awareness by giving your child the opportunity to feel a large variety of textures.

TYPES OF ATTENTION ENCOURAGED

Open and focused

MATERIALS

Items in and around your house—for example: doors, sponges, towels, rugs, throw pillows, couch, hairbrush, cotton balls, toilet paper, sink, pillow, blanket, curtains, apples, oranges, grapes, yarn, feathers, sandpaper, materials or clothes with different textures (such as silk, velvet, corduroy, wool, and tweed), trees, leaves, rocks, webbed lounge chairs

DIRECTIONS

When your child is learning to walk and enjoys taking your hand and exploring his world, it's a great time to walk around the house and yard and say, "Let's play the Feely Game. Let's see what things feel like." Then touch the refrigerator and other household items as you walk around from thing to thing.

Talk about what you are feeling and make comparisons: "That hair-brush felt rough, but this marble counter feels so smooth, doesn't it?"

You can enlarge his vocabulary by using descriptive words, such as *hard, soft, rough, smooth, bumpy, wet, dry, squishy, sharp, solid,* and so on.

VARIATIONS

♦ Make it a Temperature Tour and go around feeling the temperatures of things, such as a windowpane in winter and how that feels different from a radio that is turned on. How is the way the refrigerator feels different from the way the couch feels? Use words such as *warm, cold, ice cold, hot,* and *very hot.*

♦ Using pinking shears, cut 4-by-6-inch swatches of different fabrics, such as lace, fake fur, oilcloth, terry cloth, brocade, stretchy fabric, plain cotton, polished cotton, velvet, vinyl, and leather. Sew them together in a line and then form that line into a ring that fits around the safety belt of the car seat or stroller. Or sew squares of different textures onto a thin blanket for your child to lie on.

♦ Make a box of things to feel that he can check on at his own leisure.

WHAT'S BEING LEARNED

Toddlers are learning how to focus on the sensation of touch and to pay attention to tactile cues as they learn to distinguish between objects of different textures (or temperatures). This information will later aid them in understanding categories of textures, such as "things that are soft" and "things that are cold."

What Is That Sound?

In this game, you are making a fun activity for both an older child and his or her younger sibling. The older one gets to make the game with you, and the other gets to play it.

TYPES OF ATTENTION ENCOURAGED

Open and focused

MATERIALS

Tape recorder and tape

DIRECTIONS

With your older child, use a tape recorder to record common sounds around the house, both inside and out. Leave a pause between sounds so that your younger child knows when one has stopped and the other has started.

Here are some examples of sounds to record:

Phone ringing	Toilet flushing
Water running	Dog barking
Doorbell ringing	Car passing by
Flatware jingling	Newspaper rustling
Television turning on	Radio playing
Microwave beeping	Toaster going off
Door being knocked on	Horn honking
Piano playing	Birds chirping
Rain falling	Car starting
Washing machine or dryer running	Blender whirring
Kettle whistling	Wind chimes chiming

Once you and your older child have made the tape, one of you can play it for the younger sibling and see if she can guess what is making that sound.

VARIATION

Make the sounds yourself for your child to guess. You can imitate the sound of a horn honking, a car starting, a doorbell ringing, a dog barking, and a teapot whistling. Making the sound of a newspaper rustling, a piano playing, and some of the others may be too challenging! Make up your own variations. Can you do a tuba? Doing this variation makes it possible to play this game spontaneously, such as when walking or driving.

WHAT'S BEING LEARNED

Children are learning to focus on the various sounds in their lives and what distinguishes them from each other.

If you play the variation and your child imitates your sounds, she is also getting practice in ways of moving her tongue, lips, and jaw to make distinctive sounds. This oral-motor practice promotes good articulation and clear speech.

From Beginning to End

The ability to maintain attention from the beginning of a project to the very end is a necessary skill. You can start helping your child learn the satisfaction of a job completed even when he is very young. Here are a variety of ways to do this.

TYPE OF ATTENTION ENCOURAGED

Focused

MATERIALS

Poker chips
Yogurt container (or any container with a lid that can be slit)

DIRECTIONS

The idea of this game is to put all the chips into the yogurt container.

Slit a hole in the lid of an clean empty yogurt container. Give your child a pile of poker chips and show him how to insert them into the slit as though they were large pennies going inside a piggy bank. Have him continue adding chips until they are all inside.

VARIATIONS

♦ Clothespins and an egg carton: turn an egg carton upside down and poke holes into the cups big enough for a clothespin to stand up in. Give your child twelve clothespins and show him how to put one in each hole.

♦ Straws and a water bottle: cut up straws into two or three sections. Poke a hole in the top of the cap of a plastic water bottle. Show your learner how to fit each straw piece into the hole of the cap.

♦ Paper clips and a box: cut a slit in the top of a small box. Have your little one insert paper clips into the slit, one at a time.

There are many more possible variations to this theme. All you need is things that are small to fit into a bigger container.

WHAT'S BEING LEARNED

Children are getting an opportunity to practice focused attention in a nonchallenging activity. Even though the task of putting straws into a bottle or chips into a container is very simple, parents are continually amazed at how absorbing this activity can be, even for very little ones. I'm often also amazed at how much even much older children enjoy doing this activity. It must be that dusting-off-your-hands satisfaction of getting a job finished.

Children are also enhancing their dexterity skills, and if you have them count the number of objects as they put them in the container, they can work on their counting skills, too.

Being a Radio

Here is a game to capture your child's attention if you are stuck waiting in a car. It gives both you and your child something enjoyable to do to ease the boredom of waiting.

TYPES OF ATTENTION ENCOURAGED

Open and focused

MATERIALS

Car radio

DIRECTIONS

Keep the motor off so that the radio doesn't work, then pretend to be different stations. When your child turns the knob up, your singing gets louder. When she turns it down, your singing gets softer. When she presses a button, you sing a different song, give the weather, say the news, and so on.

Take turns being the radio and being the knob turner.

VARIATIONS

♦ Play this at home with a radio that is not plugged in and turn it into a guessing game. Pretend to turn on the radio and hum a tune that your child knows, such as "Twinkle, Twinkle Little Star" or "Itsy Bitsy Spider," and see if she can guess the song.

♦ If you have a piano or keyboard, pretend to be playing a song by striking the keys using both hands and singing a song. You don't really have to know how to play, just pretend and make sure you are singing louder than you are playing.

WHAT'S BEING LEARNED

This game is an opportunity for a fun connection between the players and is a chance to be openly creative and spontaneous. It gives children a good example of how to focus their attention with very few props. It's also a good excuse to sing favorite songs. Children don't seem to mind if you haven't got perfect pitch.

If you play the variations, you're encouraging your child's awareness of pitch and patterns, and enhancing her ability to memorize—a lot of bang for the buck.

Catch a Falling Scarf

Ball playing can be intimidating to a child just learning to coordinate his movements. It isn't so much the throwing of the ball as the trying to catch and missing that can undermine a small one's growing confidence.

Scarf catching is a great way to start feeling competent. A scarf moves so much slower than a ball that it gives wiggle room for learning.

TYPES OF ATTENTION ENCOURAGED

Open and focused

MATERIALS

Scarf

DIRECTIONS

Show your child how to throw the scarf up in the air and catch it out of the air as it floats down. Let him experiment on his own, then try tossing the scarf back and forth between you.

VARIATIONS

◆ Encourage your child to try different ways of catching. Sometimes let the scarf fall gently down into his waiting hands. Other times have him try to snatch it out of the air or jump up to get it while it is still overhead.

◆ For a whole other focusing game, blow up a balloon, hold it up for a moment to give your child time to get ready, and then let it go. As the balloon whizzes around the room, your child tries to catch it.

WHAT'S BEING LEARNED

Children are learning about timing as well as improving their eye-hand coordination. They have to pay attention to the trajectory of the falling scarf, judge when it's the right moment to catch it, and determine where their hands have to be to be successful.

Later they will transfer that awareness and timing to catching a ball.

Instant Picture

If you are going on a long car or plane ride, here is a game you might want to tuck into a plastic bag and take along.

TYPE OF ATTENTION ENCOURAGED

Focused

MATERIALS

Piece of coarse sandpaper
Bits of colored yarn

DIRECTIONS

Cut pieces of different colors of yarn in various lengths and show your child how she can stick the yarn to the sandpaper and then pull it off.

Make a design together. First, she puts down a piece of yarn and then, inspired by that placement, you add your piece next to hers. She then adds another piece to the growing design, and you both continue on until all the yarn is used up or the design feels complete.

Take all the yarn off and create another picture together or let her experiment on her own.

VARIATIONS

◆ If there are siblings or friends, provide the same materials for everyone so that the little ones can do art beside each other.

◆ You can play a similar version of this game using cooked spaghetti and a cloth place mat!

WHAT'S BEING LEARNED

Children are learning to pay attention to how the picture is forming, and they are making creative decisions on what is needed to make a pleasing design.

The endless variety makes this activity worthy of long periods of attention.

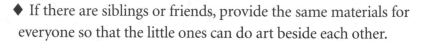

You've Got Mail

It's easy to recognize most junk mail without even needing to open it. Make a little postbox for your little one and put your junk mail in it. Let him know "You've got mail." Your child will love to open his mail while you are opening yours.

TYPE OF ATTENTION ENCOURAGED

Focused

MATERIALS

Junk mail
Shoe box
Scissors

DIRECTIONS

Make a mailbox by cutting a slot out of the top of the shoe box. Put the pieces of junk mail through the slot and let him open it.

VARIATIONS

♦ Have scissors, glue, and markers available so that he can be creative about what he does with his mail and with his mailbox.

♦ Have clean paper and envelopes available in case he wants to send out some mail himself.

WHAT'S BEING LEARNED

Children are getting the experience of dramatic play where they can try out what it would be like to have mail to read. Seeing advantages to reading encourages children to make the effort it takes to actually learn that skill.

Kaleidoscope

Children and adults love kaleidoscopes simply because watching colorful things move about, forming different exquisite patterns, is fascinating. Little ones often can't enjoy these pattern changes because they are not yet able to focus one eye through the peephole of a kaleidoscope. You can still give them that experience by making a larger version of this captivating toy.

TYPE OF ATTENTION ENCOURAGED

Focused

MATERIALS

Strong transparent plastic box
Small items, such as buttons, crinkled-up foil, feathers, glittering
    sequins, unpopped corn, colored beads, beans, broken costume
    jewelry, feathers, coins, peanuts, pebbles, salt, roofing nails
Duct tape

DIRECTIONS

Put objects in the box and tape it firmly closed.

Shake the box for your child and point out the different things inside. Your interest in the box will be infectious. After the introduction, leave the box with her to continue discovering, on her own, the ways different objects move and sound. Make sure she is not able to loosen the tape, and watch out for signs that the box is cracking as a result of the child's banging it against hard surfaces.

VARIATION

Take a clear, wide-mouth plastic bottle with a lid and fill it half full of water. If you want, add a few drops of food coloring. Put in items that float, such as corks, Ping-Pong balls, bits of sponges, and aluminum foil, and then glue or securely tape on the lid.

WHAT'S BEING LEARNED

Children are attending to the visual and auditory feedback that they cause by shaking the box. They learn that they have control over the changing of the patterns.

They also get the opportunity to visually explore small items without the danger of swallowing them.

Magnet Hunt

I often bring magnets around to the children I work with, and one of two things happens. Either they play with the magnets as if they were no different than blocks, or their eyes widen in surprise when the magnets magically and powerfully adhere to each other.

This game encourages that "Ah-ha" moment when children experience the wonder and magic of magnets.

TYPES OF ATTENTION ENCOURAGED

Open and focused

MATERIALS

One or more magnets—any kind, any shape, but the stronger the better. (Refrigerator magnets can sometimes be too weak to stick well.)

DIRECTIONS

Give your child a magnet and then go around the house with your young one as if you're going on a hunt ("Let's scout around and see if we can find things that your magnet will stick to"). Go outside and see what happens to the magnet on outside things, such as the drainpipe and the side of the house.

VARIATIONS

♦ Give your child two magnets and let him experiment with the repelling and attracting properties of the magnetic poles.

♦ Get a group of magnets and a cookie sheet and let your youngster experiment with making different designs. You could do traditional designs, such as a face with eyes, nose, mouth, ears, and hair, or some abstract designs.

♦ Place one magnet on the top of a piece of cardboard and show your child how to make it move by moving a magnet directly underneath it on the underside of the cardboard.

WHAT'S BEING LEARNED

Children are learning the properties of metal by seeing the similarities among objects to which the magnet will adhere.

They are learning how to scan their environment to look for the clues that tell them which objects are metal and therefore attracted to the magnet.

They are also focusing in on the properties of magnets themselves and how some sides will be attracted to each other and other sides will repel. This can be a fascinating discovery and can elicit long periods of concentration.

Put a Lid on It

When my godchild Nolan was fifteen months old, he was fascinated with the experience of putting the lid back on a plastic water bottle. He would fumble, drop, and persevere until he got it on right. This could be frustrating for the rest of us when he'd want to stop and practice in the middle of a vigorous hike. Still, his mother and I couldn't begrudge him his experimental learning time. For a new learner, putting lids on bottles is pretty interesting stuff that captures his attention.

Plastic bottles are almost inescapable in our lives, and whether we save them for recycling or toss them in the wastebasket, we can still get this good use out of them.

TYPE OF ATTENTION ENCOURAGED

Focused

MATERIALS

Plastic bottles in different sizes and their lids

DIRECTIONS

Give your child two or more different-size bottles and their lids. You can, for extra fun, put some tasty morsel inside, such as a raisin or chocolate chip. Show her how to rotate her wrist to unscrew the lid and then turn it the other way to screw it on. Once she gets the movements down, tighten the lid so she can also work on increasing her finger strength.

VARIATION

If your child is ready to handle glass jars, give her a variety of jars with lids. (Do this on a soft rug to avoid any breakage.) Take the lids off and toss them together, mixing them up. Now your child has the extra challenge of finding the right lid for each jar.

WHAT'S BEING LEARNED

Children are focusing on the precise and correct way to rotate their hands to screw on the lids. This is a self-correcting experience because if they've done it the right way, the lid stays on. If not, it usually falls off.

In the jar variation, children are learning to pay attention to differences in sizes and shapes as they experiment using the trial-and-error method until they choose the correct lid and it satisfyingly works!

Ooh—Smell This!

Our sense of smell needs a workout as much as our other senses, and this exercise helps a young child become more aware of this sensory equipment. Comparing whiffs helps your little one focus on similarities and differences. He might even want to share the experience with the family dog!

TYPES OF ATTENTION ENCOURAGED

Open and focused

MATERIALS

Paper cups

Aluminum foil

Variety of household substances to smell—for example: chocolate,
lemons; oranges; dill pickle; vanilla; almond; mint; anise or lemon
extract; dirt; onions; garlic; any strong-smelling spice or herb, such
as crushed basil, oregano, rosemary, curry, cilantro, and dill; pencil
shavings; vinegar; bananas; hand lotion; soap; butter; pine needles;
coffee; perfume; aftershave lotion; mouthwash; toothpaste; any
natural smells that are particular to your area, such as eucalyptus
leaves or maple syrup

DIRECTIONS

Place the various items in separate paper cups and cover each cup with aluminum foil that has small holes punched in it. Have your child try to guess
what is in each cup by smelling it. Let him peek into the cup after guessing.
Start with three different smells and then, if your child enjoys the challenge,
add more.

VARIATION

Saturate about six cotton balls (or tissue) with a variety of substances with
different smells. Place each cotton ball in a separate saltshaker or a film
canister with holes in the lid. Make two of each smell. Keep one set in front
of you and place the other set in front of your child. Sniff one shaker and
hand it to your toddler saying things like "Ooh, smell this. It smells like a
cookie!" Ask him then to smell his set to find the one that smells the same.
Continue with the rest of the smells.

Take turns smelling one of your own samples and asking the other person to find the matching smell in his set.

If your child is young, you might want to start off giving fewer choices
at first and then adding to the variations.

Talk about which smell he likes the best. Ask if any smell reminds him of something. For example, a coffee scent might remind him of the morning, and an anise smell might remind him of licorice candy.

What's Being Learned

Children are getting experience concentrating solely on one sense and beginning to distinguish and note differences and similarities between aromas.

They are using their focused attention by noticing differences in smells, which leads to an open awareness of the variety of smells around them daily.

Some children will smell everything, especially before they eat it. That lets you know that their olfactory sense is, for them, one of their strongest means of perception.

What's in the Sock?

Identifying objects with just her fingers is a skill that will absorb your child's interest and has a practical use. Think how convenient it is to have sensitive fingers when you're fumbling for a missing item in the back of a drawer.

Type of Attention Encouraged

Focused

Materials

One clean sock
Variety of small common household objects, such as a pencil, light
bulb, orange, comb, hairbrush, glue bottle, spoon, fork, or carrot

DIRECTIONS

Hide the object inside a sock. Ask your player to feel inside the sock and identify what is in it without looking inside.

VARIATIONS

♦ Have your child feel only the outside of the sock to identify what is in it.

♦ Allow your child to be the one to gather up objects and put them one by one into the sock, and you be the guesser.

WHAT'S BEING LEARNED

Children are learning to focus on the information their fingertips are sending to their brains. When they are gathering objects, they are using their open attention to scan the environment for something that is just the right size and texture.

- ~ ~ ~ ~ ~ -

PART THREE

Games for 3- to 6-Year-Olds

The world of three- to six-year-olds has expanded enormously. They have learned many fundamental skills. Their bodies follow their mental instructions; they know how to interpret sensory information. They have the beginnings of a social awareness and a concept of space, time, and sequences. Their social and physical world and their sense of what is out there have enlarged far beyond what is in their home and neighborhood to include their community and even a sense of the bigger world beyond what they've seen.

The games in this part of the book reinforce this new awareness while still helping children pay attention to what is immediately in front of them.

My Story Is the Best Story

Writing can be a challenge for children who aren't clear on how to organize their material. If children are shown when they are young the logical steps used to construct a story, they will find writing much easier as they get older.

This game gives children firsthand experience in how to plan, edit, and organize material on an always-intriguing subject: themselves.

The actual writing of the story is optional.

TYPES OF ATTENTION ENCOURAGED

Open and focused

MATERIALS

Paper and pen (optional)

DIRECTIONS

At the end of the day, encourage your child to tell you the story of his day. What happened first? What happened next? Was there a highlight? What were the various feelings that he felt at different points? Help your child tell the story by asking leading questions when appropriate, such as "What was the first thing you did when you woke up today?" "What happened next?" "Did you see anything unusual when you drove [walked] to school today?" "What was the first thing that happened when class started?" "How did that make you feel?"

VARIATIONS

♦ Ask your child to write the story down. If it seems hard to motivate your child, remind him that when he is old he will be delighted to read these stories of his youth. You can suggest that these stories could be done often and made into an autobiographical book. (Good opportunity to enlarge vocabulary here!) Or maybe there is a grandma out of town who would be thrilled to get a story about her grandson's day.

♦ Turn on the tape recorder or video camera and let your child elaborate about his day for grandparents or for posterity.

What's Being Learned

Children are learning that stories have beginnings, middles, and ends. They are seeing that there is a logical progression because they personally experienced the order of the events. When they decide which experiences to add and which to omit, they are also gaining experience with editing skills.

Children are learning open attentive skills by being aware of all the small things that happen and then focusing in on specific ones to include in the story.

If they are also encouraged to include their feelings about the various events in their day, they are learning to identify emotions.

Another Viewpoint

Have you heard the expression, "Show me a bundled-up kid and I'll show you a cold mother"? It's a reminder that our experience of the world may be different than that of our young ones. Both you and your child can benefit from being aware that others have different ways of seeing things.

My daughter Roxanne taught me about seeing another's viewpoint one day when she was about four and in one of those I-never-want-you-out-of-my-sight moods. She would start fussing the moment she couldn't see me, while her younger sister played happily beside her, never fussing at all.

Not to my credit, I got impatient and said, "You're not letting me get anything done today! Why is it that your younger sister doesn't cry when I am out of the room and you do?"

"Because," she patiently explained, "she has someone older with her!"

In this game, we all get a chance to see life from a different perspective. It can be an ant's or, if you're in a whimsical mood, that of a tiny sprite.

TYPES OF ATTENTION ENCOURAGED

Open and focused

MATERIALS

None but your imagination

DIRECTIONS

Sit outside with your little one and ask her to imagine with you that you are both tiny creatures. Look around and decide where a good place to have a home would be. Would you tuck away under the fragrant flowering bush? Or would you rather live under the gnarled tree root? Maybe you might even want to build a little home for yourselves out of rocks piled up just so.

Then look around and decide where would be a good place to play. Are you small enough to slide down that blade of grass? Would climbing up the small twig of the baby tree and then jumping off be more fun? Would you sit under that mushroom for a bit of shade or to get out of the rain?

Where would you find food to eat? What puddle has the cleanest drinking water? Continue until your child tires of the game or wants to pick a different creature to be.

VARIATION

Pick a real creature, such as an ant or a gecko, and imagine all aspects of his life.

WHAT'S BEING LEARNED

Inviting children to imagine life from a different perspective helps them begin to understand that there is more than one way of looking at situations. It expands their ability to have an open view.

You might find this works to your advantage the next time you want to reason with your child to do things your way. But then again, maybe you'll end up seeing her point of view!

Art de Deux

Collaboration in the art world is not a new practice, so why not collaborate with your little artist? Make a drawing together, each taking a turn to add a detail.

TYPES OF ATTENTION ENCOURAGED

Open and focused

MATERIALS

Pencils
Paper
Colored markers, colored pencils, crayons, or pens (optional)

DIRECTIONS

Start by drawing a person together. You draw a circle for the head and ask your fellow artist to add a body. You add arms, then he adds legs. You add fingers, then he adds toes, and so on.

You can include lots of details, such as patterns on the clothes. Does the dress have polka dots? Stripes?

Draw in the background too. Is there a tree? A house? The sun? Add color to your work by using markers, pens, crayons, or colored pencils.

You can see that this process can stay pretty simple or get fairly involved depending on the skill level and interest of the artists.

VARIATION

Take one piece of paper and fold it into four sections. The first person draws a head and face on the first section and then folds it under so that the other artist can't see the face that was drawn. The second person now draws an upper body and then folds it in such a way that neither the face nor upper body can be seen. The first artist adds the lower half of the body and then the second adds the feet.

When you're done, unfold the whole page and enjoy the resulting very mismatched person!

WHAT'S BEING LEARNED

Depending on the age of your child, he can be learning some basic information about body parts and their relationship to each other in the body.

A slightly older child may be working on copying your example and making body parts more realistic, or he may be playing around with capturing movement and expression.

No matter what their age or skill level, children are learning to focus in on the technique of drawing and opening up their imagination.

All are also getting the important message that the grown-ups in their life enjoy spending time with them. This reinforces their sense of themselves as people who are enjoyable to be with.

Batting Practice

Here's a simple activity that can keep a child amused for long periods as it increases her focusing skills and eye-hand coordination.

TYPE OF ATTENTION ENCOURAGED

Focused

MATERIALS

Ball or Wiffle ball
Rope or clothesline
Panty hose (optional)
Baseball bat or rolled-up newspaper

DIRECTIONS

Hang a ball from a low tree branch so that it's at the right height for your child to hit with a bat. If it's a plastic Wiffle ball with holes in it, it will be easy to hang with a piece of rope or clothesline. If it's a regular ball, put it inside a torn pair of panty hose and hang that.

Show your child how to bat at the hanging ball—though chances are, she'll be batting away before you even get a chance to demonstrate.

VARIATION

It doesn't have to be a ball hanging. It could be a stuffed toy of any kind. How do you think piñatas got their start?

WHAT'S BEING LEARNED

Focusing on and hitting something that's swinging enhances eye-hand coordination. Watching the trajectory of the ball when hit with different amounts of energy also elicits awareness of patterns and causality.

The Happening Book

One of the ways to help children focus on what is happening in their lives is to keep an ongoing Happening Book that records the daily, weekly, or sporadic events they've experienced.

When I was a young girl, my Happening Book was my scrapbook. Collecting for it made me notice my experiences as I was having them. Looking through it made me remember and appreciate the good moments I was having in my life.

TYPES OF ATTENTION ENCOURAGED

Open and focused

MATERIALS

Loose-leaf paper
3-ring binder
Pens
Crayons
Tape or glue
Items from the event

DIRECTIONS

Have your child record events on separate pieces of loose-leaf paper and keep them in a notebook. Give the notebook a title, such as "Kyle's Happening Book," and give each page a date and title.

There are a variety of simple methods your child can use to record an event. Let your child decide what works for him. For example, suppose your child wants to record a trip to the park. Here are some possibilities:

♦ He could draw something that happened in the park, such as Mommy and he walking hand in hand under the trees. This can be as simple as drawing stick figures or as elaborate as snipping pieces of hair and gluing them on the people in the drawing.

♦ He could glue things he found at the park, such as a flower or leaf, on the paper.

♦ He could glue something you purchased in the park, such as a popped balloon or candy wrapper, on the paper.

♦ He could cut out pictures from a brochure or magazine that has a similar feeling or look of that day and glue the pictures on the paper.

♦ He (or you, using his descriptions) could write a short story about what happened in the park. Include his emotional experience by writing down how he felt about the experience or by drawing little faces (happy, sad, mad, and so on).

VARIATIONS

♦ Instead of chronicling an event that happened, make a page about anticipated future events. For example, your child could depict the kinds of things he wants to do when he goes to visit Grandma.

♦ Instead of a Happening Book, make a Nature Book and paste in or outline things found outside, such as leaves and seeds.

WHAT'S BEING LEARNED

Happening Books encourage children to pay attention to what is happening to them and to focus on different aspects of their experiences.

Making the book encourages children to be creative and to focus on how to organize their memories.

If you ever kept a diary as a young person, you'll remember the influence it had on your day. Knowing you are going to write about your day tends to make you more aware because you want to have something to write down!

Lessons from the Rocks

I was walking along the beach one day when I spied a collection of cairns that were made and left behind. These little towers of balanced rock reminded me of an activity I was doing with a child that morning in which I was trying to help him learn about size. I had given him some measuring cups that fit inside of each other so that he would get firsthand experience of some things being bigger or smaller than others. With measuring cups, no matter how hard you try, a big cup will not fit into a smaller one.

Gathering up a small pile of different-size rocks that were more or less flat, I could see several possible games to play with your little one that will help her begin to notice differences in sizes.

TYPE OF ATTENTION ENCOURAGED

Focused

MATERIALS

Flat rocks of different sizes

DIRECTIONS

Have your child try doing these activities with the rocks:

◆ Make a Tower. Place the largest, flattest rock on the bottom and carefully add one rock after another on top. See how high she can make the tower without its falling over. You can take turns adding a rock with your child to make it a game to play together.

- ◆ Make a Line. Place the rocks in a line from largest to smallest.
- ◆ Make a Pattern. Use a variety of sizes and make a pleasing pattern with the rocks (see illustration).

End any of the games by throwing the rocks at a target, such as a larger rock, or by flinging or skipping the rocks into the sea. Or leave your cairns and rock designs for others to come upon. Maybe they will be inspired to make their own, as I had been.

WHAT'S BEING LEARNED

Children are learning to pay attention to size and shape and using the careful concentration that is needed in order to make a cairn.

If they also make a pattern, they are getting an opportunity to be creative and enter the quiet flow that creativity inspires.

If they end the game by throwing the rocks at a target, they are practicing their eye-hand coordination. If they fling them into the sea, they are developing their arm strength. If they learn how to skip a rock, they are developing arm and wrist control. These are all good ways to release any tension built up during the period of intense focusing.

Mismatched Tea Party

Pretend tea parties can be such a lovely idea, but after the "Would you like some cream?" and the "One lump or two?" teatime conversations can ebb. Mismatched cups can become "conversation pieces" and give you and yours a rich source of details to notice.

This can be the perfect game for certain grandmas to play with their grandchildren. I know I like it!

TYPES OF ATTENTION ENCOURAGED

Open and focused

MATERIALS

Mismatched teacups and saucers

DIRECTIONS

Keep an eye out at garage sales or go to secondhand stores and Asian marketplaces and look for single cups with lovely little designs on them. Your aim is to gather a small collection of inexpensive cups, each one with interesting details.

Better yet, grandma and grandchild can go on a grand shopping tour specifically to find the perfect teacups. They can explore different secondhand shops and stores together so they both can find the exact ones that catch their eye. Then they can not only have conversations about the cup's details but also reminisce about their day.

Once you've found the cups, set up a tea party table. Don't forget to invite stuffed friends and favorite dolls. This not only enlarges the guest list but also gives you an excuse to have a larger variety of cups and saucers.

Introduce conversations like the following at your next little tête-à-tête:

"Look at these little violet flowers on my cup; they're so pretty. I love that teensy dot of yellow in the middle."
"Mine has teeny roses on it like the kind Mommy grows."
"What does Teddy have on his?"
"He's got a baby octopus on his!"
"He does! I wonder what it would be like to have eight legs.
"Hmmm. How would you know which ones to cross?" (Many little ones, I've noticed, have no problem thinking that they should know the answers to everything and are quite willing to tell you.)

"Do you remember that store where we got this one? That saleslady was so funny!"

"Remember when we were eating lunch and we saw that little dog outside the window?"

VARIATION

Find interesting teaspoons, sugar bowls, milk pitchers, and so on to enliven your tea party conversation.

WHAT'S BEING LEARNED

Noticing details is the name of this game, especially zeroing in on what makes similar-looking objects different from each other. This is the skill that will later help children tell a *B* from a *D* or an isosceles triangle from an acute one.

At the same time, it opens the child's awareness to the many patterns that are possible.

Plenty Peanut Hunt

Easter hunts can be such fun if there are plenty of eggs so everyone finds a lot. It's not fun to have "egg envy" looking at someone else's brimming-over basket.

That's why in this fun hunt game, competition is eliminated, as there are plenty of peanuts to find and eat!

TYPES OF ATTENTION ENCOURAGED

Open and focused

MATERIALS

Plenty of roasted peanuts in the shell or other small treats. (Keep in mind the age and propensities of the child; a toddler who still puts things in her mouth wouldn't do well finding marbles, nor should the child allergic to nuts be sent on a peanut hunt.)

Baskets or bags.

DIRECTIONS

Hide peanuts all over, inside and out. Put some in obvious places such as right out on the lawn or carpet, and hide some away in sneakier places for the older hunters. The goal is for everyone to find lots of nuts and share them at the end if they want.

VARIATION

Use wrapped hard candies, fake coins, poker chips, marbles, Popsicle sticks, or anything else that is safe for your child to find and won't be harmed by the weather or tramping feet.

WHAT'S BEING LEARNED

Hunters are exercising their open attention skills as they scan the areas for peanuts or other items. Looking closely in specific places enhances their focusing skills.

Playing a hunting game right alongside everyone else—sharing a goal and being successful—highlights children's social skills. They belong because they are one part of a whole group!

Regroup Time

It may be a bit of a stretch to call Regroup Time a game when it sounds suspiciously like "time-out," but there is a big difference. Time-out has come to feel like a punishment, so it's not something to use when children need more understanding about what they are experiencing. Regroup time gives the child a break from the action and time to soothe and refresh his body and soul.

TYPE OF ATTENTION ENCOURAGED

Focused

MATERIALS

Whatever your child likes to do for a little quiet time (see suggestions below)

DIRECTIONS

When things get too much for your youngster and his actions and emotions get disorganized and out of control, suggest that it's time to regroup. Let him know you understand that he's not being bad—he's just having a difficult time. You could say something like "Do you need some time to get yourself together?" or "Why don't you go and cool down for a while and come join us when you're ready" or "This feels like a good time to go to your special spot."

Set up a place ahead of time that has the ingredients that work for your child. Would he like art supplies, books, music or story CDs, a yoga mat with photos of yoga poses to imitate? Let him help you set up his spot and help pick the activities that interest him.

This quiet place of renewal can be under a table or out in the yard or in a cozy chair set up in a quiet corner. It is not in front of the television. The idea is not to distract but to soothe with an activity that will make your child feel better about himself and teach him a creative method of calming down that will serve him his whole life.

VARIATIONS

Teach your child this self-calming technique of taking deep breaths and consciously calming himself.

1. Say to yourself "I'm calming down."

2. Count to five slowly.

3. Take three deep breaths with one hand on your belly so that you can feel it rise on the in-breath.

Practice it yourself and show it to your little one when he is already calm. Rehearse it more than once on different days. This way, when fears, anger, and anxieties come up, he'll already have a method for dealing with them.

When children have excess energy and need large motor movements to release it, jumping on a mini-trampoline or punching a punching bag or running outside can be a way of regrouping.

WHAT'S BEING LEARNED

Children are learning self-calming skills. When we are angry or confused or we lose control, we can go to a quiet place to sort things out and make ourselves feel better. This will put us in a better frame of mind to deal with the problem.

Because this is a life lesson everyone needs, it is also helpful if children see you doing something similar when you are feeling frustrated or angry. "I'm feeling frustrated now and need some regroup time. I'm going to go write in my journal for a while. I'll be back when I've calmed myself down."

Shadow Games

Shadows make instant fun. The next time you are outside with your darling child when the sun is low on the horizon, have good fun romping with these games.

TYPE OF ATTENTION ENCOURAGED

Focused

MATERIALS

None

DIRECTIONS

♦ Don't Step on My Shadow. Telling your child not to do something that she knows is really okay to do makes this game silly fun. You say, "Don't step on my shadow" and keep scurrying away as she tries to put a foot on your shadow. Take turns with this one, letting her tell you what not to do!

♦ Can You Make My Shape? Take a position, such as arms out to the side, and ask your child to make her shadow look exactly like yours. Keep changing shapes as well as imitating the shapes she makes.

VARIATIONS

Create shadows on the wall in a dark room with only one light on. Take a pose and have the child imitate that pose by looking only at your shadow and not at you. Take turns creating the shadows. Give the poses names if you want.

WHAT'S BEING LEARNED

Children's attention is captured by the situation and then sustained through imitation and challenge.

Deck of Cards

Don't underestimate the fascination of a deck of cards to a child just getting interested in recognizing numbers and sorting colors and shapes. I had one little friend who was so enamored of his card deck that he spent hours sorting the suits and putting the cards in order according to number. He even insisted that the cards lay beside him at night. (His parents started to get concerned, but after a week he was on to something else.) I noted what a great learning tool and attention grabber a deck of cards could be.

TYPE OF ATTENTION ENCOURAGED

Focused

MATERIALS

Deck of cards; if the cards also have beautiful pictures or interesting patterns on one side, so much the better

DIRECTIONS

Bring out the deck and just show your child the different aspects of the cards. Name the suits and point out how the written numbers correspond with the actual amount of objects. "The five of hearts is suppose to have five hearts on it—let's count and see if that's true: 1-2-3-4-5. It *is* true!"

Offer to sort the cards with him according to suit or color, or put them in order from ace to king. If he'd like it, give him the box of cards to keep in a special place and to play with whenever he wants.

VARIATIONS

♦ Introduce simple card games, such as War, to help children understand that some numbers represent larger numbers than others.

♦ Introduce Go Fish to point out the similarities between colors and numbers.

♦ If your child doesn't seem interested in playing a game, just sit yourself down and play a game of solitaire. There is nothing that spurs a child's interest in something more than seeing his grown-up having fun with it.

WHAT'S BEING LEARNED

Children are learning to pay attention to how some things are similar and some things are different—for example, spades and clubs both being black but having different shapes.

They are also getting practice in putting things in order from ace to king and separating the cards according to color or suit.

Incidentally, this is an opportunity to notice how close or how far your child holds the cards to look at them. If he holds the cards very close or far away from his eyes, it could be a clue that he needs glasses.

Hand on Top

One of the things we want our little ones to know is that interaction with others is interesting and that other people are worth their attention. The interaction doesn't necessarily have to be big fun to get your child's attention; pleasant small moments give the same message. Here is an example of a small fun moment that you might have experienced in your younger life.

TYPE OF ATTENTION ENCOURAGED

Focused

MATERIALS

None

DIRECTIONS

Put your hand on the table and ask your little one to put hers on top of yours. Then put your other hand on top of her hand and ask her to put her other hand on the top of the hand pile.

Then you pull your first hand out from under the pile of hands and put it back on top. Encourage her to do the same with her hand that is now on the bottom.

Keep repeating this pattern with the hand on the bottom of the pile moving to the top. Start very slowly at first until your child gets the idea and then begin to speed up the action.

VARIATION

Try the same game with your bare feet!

WHAT'S BEING LEARNED

Children are learning about taking turns, a concept that will stand them well in preschool and beyond.

They are also learning about timing. If they pull their hand out too soon, the game doesn't work.

They are also learning about simple ways to enjoy themselves with others.

How Many?

Everyone has trouble waiting, but especially fidgety children. In this game, you can turn waiting for someone to come pick you up or for someone to get off a plane into a fun guessing game.

TYPES OF ATTENTION ENCOURAGED

Open and focused

MATERIALS

None

DIRECTIONS

Everyone who is waiting takes a guess on how many cars will pass before the right one stops or how many people will get off the plane until the right person arrives.

Whoever is right gets the satisfaction of being right, and everyone gets the fun of seeing who is closest.

VARIATION

If everyone's number has passed and still the car or person hasn't shown up, guess again!

WHAT'S BEING LEARNED

This game shows children a way of making a potentially uncomfortable situation fun by focusing their attention on guessing and counting.

It also helps little ones with their counting skills!

Indoor Picture Hunt

This is a fun scavenger hunt game that shows little ones that pictures are symbols for real objects.

TYPES OF ATTENTION ENCOURAGED

Open and focused

MATERIALS

Magazine pictures or drawn pictures

DIRECTIONS

Cut out magazine pictures, draw pictures, or actually photograph and print pictures of things around the house, such as a lamp, couch, refrigerator, and the like.

Hide the pictures around the house for the child to find so that one picture clue leads to another. For example, your child is handed Picture Clue 1, which is a picture of a lamp. He finds the lamp, and taped on the back of the lamp is Picture Clue 2, which is a picture of a couch. The final clue should lead to a hidden treasure, such as a tasty treat or a new ball or book.

VARIATIONS

◆ If your child is learning to read, you might want to use words rather than pictures.

◆ This idea can be a good treasure hunt game for a birthday party. Place the clues outside and a good distance from each other. Children will gleefully run from clue to clue, burning off that birthday cake sugar!

WHAT'S BEING LEARNED

Children are learning about symbols by matching a picture to a real item.

They are also learning about sequencing and that things need to happen in a certain order—first this, then this, then this, and so on. This is a skill that children need every day. For example, whether they are brushing their teeth or getting dressed or making a mud pie, they need to make things happen in a certain order to be successful.

Children are also learning to persevere with a task until it is completed and the reward achieved. Remember, a reward doesn't have to be material; it could be a walk to the playground with Daddy.

Mexican Yo-Yo

If you are up for making a toy out of yesterday's empty bleach bottle, this is an easy one to make and will give your little one some focused entertainment.

The original Mexican yo-yo is a stick with a cup and a ball on a string attached to it. The player has to swing the ball into the cup. It's not always easy to do.

In this easier homemade version for little children, the cup is much bigger, and so is the ball.

TYPE OF ATTENTION ENCOURAGED

Focused

MATERIALS

Clean empty bleach bottle
12-inch length of string
Sponge or Wiffle ball

DIRECTIONS

Cut the bottom section, below the handle, off the bleach bottle. Unscrew the lid of the bottle, place one end of the string inside the bottle, and screw the lid back on. The lid squashes the string in place. The majority of the string hangs down from the lid. Attach a Wiffle ball or sponge to the end of this hanging string (see illustration).

Have the player hold the bleach bottle upside down by the handle, with the open end facing up. She should then move the bottle so that the ball swings out and up, and try to catch the ball in the open end of the bleach bottle.

VARIATION

If the bleach bottle game is too easy for your child, make it more of a challenge by using a detergent bottle for the cup and a scrunched-up piece of aluminum foil for the ball.

WHAT'S BEING LEARNED

To be successful in this game, children have to pay attention to their muscles so that they can modify how wildly or softly they swing the ball to accomplish the goal. It takes concentration to notice which movements cause which result—a good lesson in focusing, and instant positive feedback if they get it right!

Mini-Montessori

One feature of the Montessori method of teaching young people is to have learning projects available that children, once they have been given proper instructions, are allowed to pursue in their own time. These projects are kept on shelves and are continually available.

When my children were very young, I had fun making a mini-Montessori area in their bedroom. I placed a variety of homemade projects on shelves and would change the projects from time to time to capture and keep their interest.

It doesn't take any skill to do this, just an enjoyment of making things with your hands and a willingness to gather up the necessary materials.

Here are examples of seven projects to put on the shelves of a preschool child. I put each one on a small tray to keep the material contained. If I don't have enough trays, I'll clean and use those Styrofoam trays that are often used to package meat in grocery stores. (Note that true Montessorians would never use Styrofoam because they prefer something more esthetically pleasing. I truly appreciate that, but sometimes have to make do with what I have.)

TYPE OF ATTENTION ENCOURAGED

Focused

MATERIALS

See individual projects

DIRECTIONS
Project 1: Color Matching with a Paper Clip Bank

(Note: This project is only for children who no longer put small objects in their mouth.)

Small cardboard box with lid (such as a gift box)
Colored paper clips
Knife

Glue a paper clip of each color to the top of the cardboard box. Beside each color, slash a small slit, big enough for a paper clip to fit through. Place this box and the box of paper clips on a tray.

Your child's job is to take the paper clips, one by one, and put them through the slit next to the clip with the matching color. This activity increases his awareness of color as well as improves his dexterity.

Project 2: Nesting Measuring Cups

Measuring cups

Place a set of measuring cups on a tray and encourage your learner to take them apart and replace them in the right order so that they nest into each other. This activity teaches an awareness of sizes.

Project 3: Spooning

Two small bowls
One small spoon
Rice

Place two bowls next to each other. Put rice in the bowl on the left. The child's job is simply to spoon all the rice from the bowl on the left to the one on the right. Going from left to right prepares him for eventually reading from left to right.

Spooning so that no (or very little) rice spills encourages your child's ability to be careful and precise.

Project 4: Drawing on Stone

Smooth, flat rock about the size of a small hand
Paintbrush
Small container with water

Put the rock, paintbrush, and small container of water on a tray.

The temporary nature of painting with water on rock encourages experimentation with creative drawing skills.

Project 5: Putting Things in Order

Magnetic numbers or letters
Cookie sheet

Put the magnetic numbers or letters on a cookie sheet. Your child's job is to put the numbers or letters in the right order. For young children, start by using only the numbers one through six and later add more.

Project 6: Money in the Bank

(Note: If your child might put small objects in his mouth, use poker chips instead of the coins and a large yogurt container with a slit in its lid.)

Coins
Container (for example, clean, empty margarine tub) with slit cut in
     the lid

Fill a saucer with coins and place that on a tray next to the container with a slit on the top. Your child's job is to put all the coins in the slot.

Project 7: Hammering

Block of Styrofoam (such as the ones that come in boxes for shipping
     computers)
Small hammer (tack hammers work well)
Nails or golf tees

Put the block of Styrofoam, a saucer of nails or golf tees, and a small hammer on a tray, and you've got an activity young children love: hammering all the tees or nails into the Styrofoam.

Project 8: Eyedropping

Eyedropper
Two small containers
Water
Food coloring (optional)

Put an eyedropper and two small containers on a tray. Put water in one container and show your learner how to use the eyedropper to move the water from one container to the other.

Add food coloring to the water if you'd like.

VARIATIONS

Anything that strikes your fancy that is safe, fun to do, and doesn't need batteries!

WHAT'S BEING LEARNED

Children are developing their ability to concentrate and focus on one activity from start to finish.

Along the way they are picking up information and making connections about size, color, letters, and numbers, as well as enhancing their creativity and finger dexterity.

Going on a Monster Hunt

Do you remember being afraid of night monsters? I do. I even had a plan for dealing with them. I would trick them! I'd crawl under the covers to the foot of the bed, fix up a little air hole, curl up, and start meowing. I figured any monster looking for a child would say, "Oh, that's just a bunch of little kittens—who wants those? I want a little girl, but I guess there are none here, so I'll go away."

I think it worked. It was better than grown-ups' saying there weren't any monsters around and then turning on the light to prove it. That made it worse because it meant monsters knew how to disappear!

The following game respects a child's fear by doing something practical about it.

TYPE OF ATTENTION ENCOURAGED

Open

MATERIALS

(All optional)
Pillow
Flashlight
Broom

DIRECTIONS

When your child expresses fear of nighttime monsters, go on a monster hunt with her. Walk around the room together looking in closets, under blankets, and behind chairs. Stomp your feet behind the chair, thump a pillow on the tumbled blankets, and make threatening sounds in the closet. Do anything you would both enjoy to let any possible monsters understand who is in charge here. This can include taking a flashlight and going around the house, shaking a broom or a fist, and telling any monsters who might even *think* about coming this way to move on!

VARIATION

If your child is the kind who would rather chase rainbows than monsters, you might try another approach. I did when my daughter, Marissa, was four years old and feeling wary of monsters in the night.

"I hope they didn't hear you say you're were scared of them," I told her.

"Why?" she asked.

"Because it might hurt their feelings. If there really are monsters, they must have a terrible time making friends. Every time they go anywhere, people run away from them. It must be a hard life."

"I love you, monsters," she said.

She knew. Everyone needs love.

WHAT'S BEING LEARNED

Children are fully attentive when their very real fears are being heard and dealt with, just as we adults are very attentive when someone is listening and helping us deal with our problems.

We are teaching our children to pay attention to how they feel and to find creative ways of dealing with their fears.

Paint the World

If you've ever painted large surfaces, you know how absorbing and calming it can be. You can give children this experience without mess or permanent change by letting them paint the world with water.

TYPES OF ATTENTION ENCOURAGED

Open and focused

MATERIALS

Large paintbrushes
Pail of water

DIRECTIONS

Let your child use the water to paint a large area, such as the outside of your house or a fence. The water temporarily darkens any area it covers, giving the illusion of change.

VARIATIONS

♦ If a bit of water on the floor doesn't bother you, use a roller paintbrush on a bathroom wall.

♦ If there is a fence or playhouse that is okay for children to really paint, use a variety of paint colors to keep the attention high and results colorful. (House painters often have a lot of leftover paints from jobs they've finished.)

WHAT'S BEING LEARNED

Children's attention is being engaged by the fascination of changing the look of a large area.

As an added benefit, they are also getting to stretch their bodies to reach high places and strengthen their arm muscles with the repetitive motion.

The Perfect Gifts

Finding the right gift for your child can be wearing. I found that if I didn't think of something ahead of time, I'd wander around a toy store looking for something to catch my eye and then get caught by expensive stuff that was not quite right.

Because I also work with children and often need to find interesting materials to capture their interest and encourage their development, I got in the habit of looking for potential gifts wherever I went. Often the perfect gift would not be in the toy store but in the hardware store!

TYPES OF ATTENTION ENCOURAGED

Open and focused

MATERIALS

Any of the items in the gift sets described below, plus boxes and wrapping supplies

DIRECTIONS

Gift 1

Business supplies may mean work to us workers, but to a child they are a great source of play. Buy things like paper clips, a stapler, a hole puncher, folding files, index cards, a ledger, tape, a ruler, sticky notes, a receipt book with carbon paper, tracing paper, stamp pads, stamps, graph paper, colored stickers, and highlighters. Store them in an empty boot box (free at any shoe store), which will serve as a lap desk as well as a supply box. This assortment of interesting stuff will keep kids busy for hours, and isn't that what "busi-ness" is all about anyway?

Gift 2

If your child is old enough to use a needle safely, buy or assemble from your own supplies a box of cotton or a bag of cotton balls, scraps of material, and needle and thread to make small pillows for dolls or stuffed animals.

Sometimes children just like to plunge their hands into all that softness or paste it on pictures to make clouds or beards.

Gift 3

Embroidery threads are great for the budding or advanced embroiderer. You could get one skein of every color, a hoop, some large-eye needles, and a beautiful small box with drawers to put them in.

Gift 4

An all-purpose cape is great. If you are good at sewing, make a cape out of old velvet or glossy satin or some other spectacular material so your child can be Superman or a prince or Cinderella or a sorceress or a wizard. If you don't sew, secondhand stores are also good for finding dramatic clothes and gobs of gaudy costume jewelry.

Gift 5

Assemble a collection of shoe boxes. Shoe stores often have a slew of empty shoe boxes that their customers didn't want. The regular-size ones make wonderful trains for a younger child. You could connect some boxes with a piece of string running through them, leaving a longer piece at the front for pulling. You can add wheels, paint it, put animals inside, and so on.

Shoe boxes with lids and larger boot boxes can be decorated by collaging or painting and personalized to make a private place for your child's treasures.

Gift 6

A magnifying glass is something no self-respecting five-year-old should be without. Add a length of yarn and turn a small magnifying glass into a necklace. I gave that to my child when she was five, and she wore it constantly for weeks, checking out the whole world, up close and personal.

Gift 7

A ream of paper and a package of colored felt-tip pens is a dream gift. I can't imagine an up-and-coming artist, writer, or scribbler alive who wouldn't love five hundred sheets of paper and a package of pens all her own!

Gift 8

An assortment of colored ribbons can win a girl's heart. Get a yard of each of several colors and in a variety of materials, such as satin, velveteen, and woven fibers. Then get a floral tin (or decorate a shoe box) to put them in, along with a small pair of scissors.

Gift 9

Fill a tackle box or toolbox with a collection of small toys and other fun and unusual items. (I have found interesting items in the toy section of import shops.) Here are some examples:

Modeling clay
Spinning top
Package of farm animals
Package of craft sticks
Bottle of bubble solution
Squirting water toy

I did this for my twin grandsons when they were three years old and labeled the box "Mama's Five-Minute Break Box." When Mom needed some time to herself, she could pull one of these items from the box and "take five." The boys were equally delighted with the gear box!

Gift 10

My late husband would stop twice yearly at a large Salvation Army store and ask for their broken costume jewelry. They would always give him a large bag full, and our daughters found this an unending treasure of decorative possibilities.

Gift 11

Of course, you can never go wrong buying your children books. It's impossible to overestimate the importance of books in a child's development. A child who is read to develops vocabulary and language more easily, has a larger sense of the world around her, and, most important, feels cared for. If you want to give your children true wealth, read to them.

VARIATIONS

Find variations any time you go into a store that is *not* a toy store. Look around and think, "Would my child enjoy playing with this object (and would she be safe)?" For example, I saw some little toddler socks on sale that were cheap and colorful. I bought them, filled them with sand, knotted off the top and drew a face on the toe. They were great for throwing at targets and for an easy game of toss.

WHAT'S BEING LEARNED

There are a thousand chances to be creative and imaginative with these materials, and they all encourage long periods of focused and open attention.

Creativity is the open ability to look at many aspects of familiar materials and put them together in new ways. Imagination is the ability of the mind to conceive ideas or to form images of something not present to the senses or within the actual experience of the person involved.

A child who focuses on decorating her cape with ribbons, cotton balls, and bits of costume jewelry and pretends to be the Grand Wizard is being both creative *and* imaginative!

Sounds Right

With just a little preparation, you can play this game that enhances your little one's attention and hearing skills. All you need are some film canisters and some household materials.

TYPE OF ATTENTION ENCOURAGED

Focused

MATERIALS

8 empty film canisters (free at photo developing stores) or clean, empty, opaque pill bottles or toilet paper tubes, with the ends covered with tape and paper or foil

4 small household items, such as salt, rice, coins, buttons, pasta, sand, pebbles, or dried peas, lentils, or beans

DIRECTIONS

Fill two of the film canisters with one of the items, such as salt. Continue to fill pairs of canisters with different materials. Your child can help with the preparation and get some experience with pouring as well as have the fun of doing a project together.

Place one of each pair of filled canisters on the table in front of each of you.

To begin the game, first have him shake one of his containers; then you shake each of yours until you find the one that makes the same sound.

Next, you shake one of yours, and he shakes each one of his until he finds the right sound.

Remember to put the identified canisters back in with the others after each turn so that neither of you can use the process of elimination.

VARIATIONS

You can make this game as hard or as easy as appropriate for your child. Start by playing with the containers that are distinctly different, such as

salt, pennies, and beans, and keep adding more similar ones as he gets better and better at distinguishing the differences in sound. For example, to
make the game harder, fill some containers with sugar or sand, which
sound a lot like salt. Containers with pennies and dimes sound more similar than pennies and nickels.

All done playing? Make music! Use the containers as shakers and keep
the beat to any song that comes into your head. Sing it loud and together,
and shake away!

WHAT'S BEING LEARNED

Auditory discrimination is the name of the skill being learned, but there's
more to this game than that. Children's ability to listen and focus on what
they hear is strengthened. This ability takes a concentrated shift of attention
and is important in a wide range of activities, whether it's distinguishing
between bird songs or really paying attention to what someone else is saying.

Word Matching

*As your little one discovers the world of words, here is a simple game you
can make together that she can play for long periods alone. You can keep
adding to her deck of cards, enlarging her own personal treasury of words.*

TYPE OF ATTENTION ENCOURAGED

Focused

MATERIALS

Index cards
Pen

DIRECTIONS

Start with ten plain index cards and, together with your potential reader,
come up with five words she would want to be able to read. It could be the

names of all the family members, the names of interesting things in the room, the names of pets (I know one four-year-old who loves the names of the planets), and so on.

Write each of the five words on two index cards so that there are two sets of cards. Later you'll add more word cards.

Lay one set of the cards out on the table with the word facing up.

Give the second set of cards to your player and ask her to find the matching word and put her card on top of it. Say the word as she puts it down. She doesn't need to be able to read the words to recognize the similarities in the shapes.

VARIATION

Lay out both sets of cards face down on the table. Players take turns flipping over cards two at a time to find the matching sets.

WHAT'S BEING LEARNED

Children are focusing on the ways words and letters differ from each other visually. They are becoming comfortable with the written language as common words become familiar and easy to recognize.

As the child's pile of familiar words grows, so will the child's sense of herself as a person who can read.

PART FOUR

Games for 6- to 12-Year-Olds

The ages of six through twelve are a time when children are leaving the little kid's world and starting to try on some of the skills they will need for their adulthood. In school they are reading, writing, developing their math skills, learning more about the wider world, and socializing. Because this is the age when children are becoming increasingly aware of being part of a much larger world than their family and neighborhood, they are also more aware of their ability to fit into this world. They are noticing which skills they have and perhaps experiencing some anxiety about the skills they don't have. As we know from our own experience, anxieties directly affect our ability to pay attention.

The games in this part of the book help children develop needed skills, such as reducing anxieties, managing time, noticing details, engaging in hobbies, increasing dexterity, reading maps, and even reading faces. Yet kids are still kids, so these games teach grown-up skills in a fun way that will appeal to their child's heart.

All the Things You Can Think Of

A good way to get the brain moving is to give it a workout. Besides exercising the brain, this game could help pass frustrating time during a traffic jam.

TYPE OF ATTENTION ENCOURAGED

Open

MATERIALS

None

DIRECTIONS

Take turns asking, "What are all the things you can think of that . . . ?" Fill in the blank with whatever you like; here are some possibilities:

. . . start with the letter __?
. . . you can buy at a fair?
. . . are the names of states?
. . . live in the jungle?
. . . live on the prairie?

Pick topics that are interesting to your players, such as characters from their favorite TV shows or video games or players on their favorite sports team. This is not a test, but it can be a chance to show off.

VARIATION

Instead of things, ask for people in their lives:

"Who are the people at your school?"
"Who are the people who have come over to our house?"
"Who are your relatives?"

WHAT'S BEING LEARNED

This game requires that children scan their memories for experiences to find the connections among many things.

It takes concentration for a long period and can provide a sense of pride in one's vast knowledge.

Asking questions about people they know gives children a chance to broaden their view of the world by making them aware of all the different people they come in contact with.

Back Writing

Writing invisible letters on a child's back is a game that can be played to help young children learn letters. But it's also a fun way for older children to write a secret message.

TYPE OF ATTENTION ENCOURAGED

Focused

MATERIALS

Paper and pencil

DIRECTIONS

One person sits with his back to another and a pad of paper and pencil in front of him.

The other person, using her finger, "draws" a letter on the person's back.

At the same time, that person draws on the paper what he thinks is being drawn on his back.

Keep writing letter by letter until a whole message is given.

Take turns so that both the writer and the person written on get to experience what it feels like.

VARIATIONS

Have an older child play this game with a younger sibling as a fun way to help the younger child learn his letters.

You could also have the message be a clue to where a treat is hidden!

WHAT'S BEING LEARNED

Children are learning to pay close attention to tactile information and to integrate that sensation with their academic knowledge.

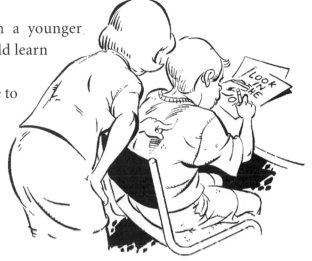

Belly Counts

As long as we are practicing our focusing skills, why not get buff at the same time? With this game of conscious isometrics, children can not only lengthen their focusing skills but also get "killer abs" if they play often enough. (So will you, if you do it with them!)

TYPE OF ATTENTION ENCOURAGED

Focused

MATERIALS

None

DIRECTIONS

Have your child hold in her stomach muscles and start counting. Be sure she keeps breathing. The idea is to stay focused on keeping the stomach muscles taut and not get distracted. See what number she can count to before she gets distracted or her muscles tire. Then, after a small break, try again.

VARIATION

Up the challenge by seeing if your child can do the exercise while continuing to do her regular routine, such as doing homework, taking a walk, or doing dishes. Can part of her attention stay on the tightened abdominal? For how long?

WHAT'S BEING LEARNED

Tightening any muscle takes concentration. Children need to be aware of what they are doing *while* they are doing it.

The more children practice their skill of staying focused in any area, the more likely that skill is to spill over to other areas.

Expanding Interest

Watching our children try out new interests, we start to notice patterns. We might notice that one child always likes to tinker with machines; another spends long periods drawing; yet another seems most content playing with the family pet.

In this activity, we take notice of these interests and provide the means for these interests to expand.

TYPES OF ATTENTION ENCOURAGED

Open and focused

MATERIALS

See suggestions below

DIRECTIONS

Notice which activities tend to engage your child's interest, and think of various ways to expand that interest. Discuss your ideas with your child and brainstorm together to see if any of the ideas cause him to light up or if he has some ideas of his own. Then put your ideas into practice. Here are some examples:

◆ For the child who likes to pretend to play the guitar

Instead of just letting him play "air guitar," ask if he would like to learn how to play for real. You may find that a music studio is best for lessons, or you can find a local person who would be interested in giving your child private lessons.

◆ For the child who likes to draw cartoons

Ask your child if she would like a workbook on how to draw cartoon figures that breaks the process down into easy-to-understand procedures. Go online or to a local bookstore together to find one.

Is it possible to visit a studio in your area that creates cartoons?

◆ For the child who loves to play with the family pets

Ask your child if he'd like to visit the local veterinarian. If the child is older, you might even ask the vet if your child could work as an intern for a while. Interns may not get paid and may have the clean-up-the-poop jobs, but for an animal lover, it might be heaven.

◆ For the child who used to love making mud patties and now enjoys making figures in the sand when she's at the beach

See if there is a local shop or home where people can make clay projects that are fired in their kiln. Go together and try it out. You can also buy oil-based sculpting clay that doesn't need firing or the kind that can be "fired" in a regular oven.

◆ For the child who enjoys helping you cook

Find a recipe book that is just right for his age. After he selects the first recipe and makes a list of ingredients, go buy them together.

VARIATIONS

Unending. Keep in mind that as your child grows, her interests might change. Her interest in cartooning, for example, may expand into a different art form requiring pastels, watercolor, or oil painting. Or she may have satisfied her interest in art for now and has a completely different interest. Stay tuned.

WHAT'S BEING LEARNED

Children are learning that they can be open to a wide variety of possible interests and learning how to focus on specific ones.

- ~ - ~ - ~ - ~ - ~ - ~ - ~ - ~ - ~ - ~ - ~

Focused Fidgeting

Some of us are born fidgeters. We gnaw on pencils, drum our fingers, tap our feet, pace or doodle when we are on the phone. There's nothing wrong with fidgeting, and it doesn't mean your child is not paying attention. It's an effective way of releasing excess tension. If your child has that need, here's a way to honor it by giving him something that is infinitely malleable—sculpting clay.

It could help him deal with such situations as sitting still and listening in the classroom.

TYPES OF ATTENTION ENCOURAGED

Open and focused

MATERIALS

Sculpting clay (oil-based clay found at hobby shops, school supply stores, and variety stores)

DIRECTIONS

Give a small piece of sculpting clay to your learner and suggest he play with it when he is required to sit quietly. Sculpting clay is oil based, so it never dries out. It can be twisted, squished, flattened, and rolled and is always satisfyingly responsive to all poking and pulling.

VARIATIONS

There are other small items that can be used as fidget tools that won't be distracting. A balloon filled with cornstarch can have a calming effect when squeezed. Keep an eye out for other possibilities, such as interlocking rings and plastic frogs with stretchy limbs.

WHAT'S BEING LEARNED

In order to pay attention, some children need to deal first with the anxiousness that is the natural by-product of stress. Fidget items respect the child's need to release excess energy and give him a subtle and satisfying way to do it. He is learning to identify and deal with that anxious energy that will probably come up many times in his life. Knowing what works for him will help him find other ways that are effective too.

And, who knows, if he chooses clay, he may be launching a focused sculpting career!

Guess How Old

Children seem to hit an age when they are suddenly curious about other people's ages, but they don't yet know what clues to notice. I had this experience as a seven-year-old when my piano teacher, on her birthday, wanted me to guess her age. I figured I was seven and she was older, so I said innocently, "Seventy?" Much to my surprise, she huffed up and walked out the door. (What did I say?)

Much, much later, I was talking to a seven-year-old who wanted to know my age. She began to guess my age: "Twenty?" (no); "Fifty?" (no); "Thirty?" (no). "I'm sixty," I said. "Oh," she said, "My grandma is sixty, and I thought you were older." Right before I started to feel like an obvious wrinkled-up mess, I asked her how she knew I was older. "Because you are taller," she replied.

In this game, you'll help your child pay attention to clues that indicate age.

TYPES OF ATTENTION ENCOURAGED

Open and focused

MATERIALS

None

DIRECTIONS

While sitting all cuddled up with your child, play the game of Guess How Old by letting her guess the ages of people and animals in your life, people in the neighborhood, people on television, or even the characters in books. How old are the Cat in the Hat, Big Bird, and Barney, anyway? How old are the nearby trees? Make a guess. Explain why you think someone or something is young or old.

It might interest your little guesser that some of our winged friends live for only one day, whereas trees can live for hundreds of years. If you happen to have a tree stump nearby, you can show her how to count the rings.

WHAT'S BEING LEARNED

Children are learning that there is a progression of development and that we all, even trees, have stages we go through as we age.

They also learn to pay attention to the details that give us a sense of how old people or animals or trees are. This increases children's awareness of others and gives them other clues to notice.

How Do You Look?

Reading body language and facial expression is not a course one can take at school, yet it's a big part of our daily life curriculum.

I play this game with groups of children, and they can't wait to have a turn to make a face and movement that express an emotion. Try it with your child or with the family at the dinner table.

TYPE OF ATTENTION ENCOURAGED

Open

MATERIALS

None

DIRECTIONS

Take turns making a face and gesture that depict these feelings:

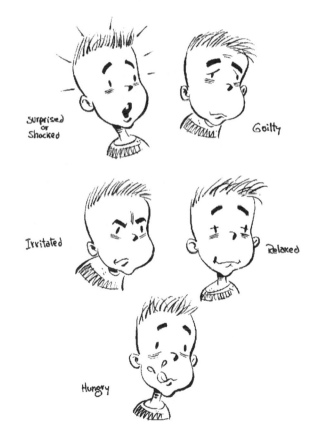

Stuck-up	Relieved
Disgusted	Confused
Frightened	Shocked
Proud	Hungry
Shy	Angry
Giddy	Powerful
Guilty	Surprised
Goofy	Impatient
Lonely	Relaxed
Irritated	Anxious

VARIATIONS

♦ One person picks an emotion and acts it out. The other(s) have to guess the emotion.

♦ One person goes from one emotion to another in quick succession.

WHAT'S BEING LEARNED

Children are enlarging their ability to be aware of body language, their own and others'. They are learning to be attentive to social cues.

They are also learning that you can pay attention and still be silly and giggle with others.

Junk Box Art

This project may not appeal to everyone, but it's perfect for the "pack rats" among us who tend to collect bits and pieces of random stuff. If you or your child is drawn to collecting intriguing shells, odd buttons, colorful fabric swatches, occasional buckles, interesting pebbles, bits of colored yarn, pretty pipe cleaners, and broken jewelry too lovely to throw away, you can use all these things as fabulous art material.

Making something out of a lot of different nothings is a lovely way to spend a pleasant rainy day.

TYPES OF ATTENTION ENCOURAGED

Open and focused

MATERIALS

Any kind of found art material: buttons, yarn, sea shells, and so on
Variety of household items to decorate: gift box, hat, cardboard, and
    the like
Glue

DIRECTIONS

As these types of materials appear in your life, place them in a shoe box. When the mood and moment seem right, bring the box out for your young one to "ooh and ah" over as you examine each item. Then let his imagination loose in thinking about how he can use these items to decorate something around the house.

For example, a bottle of glue and a piece of cardboard can turn these treasures into a collage. A wooden cigar box or gift box covered with these objets d'art becomes a unique treasure box. Feathers and yarn and fabric swatches can make an old hat into a new designer creation. Pipe cleaners and buttons can be transformed into a one-of-a-kind bracelet.

The possible art projects are endless, and it all begins with your propensity for collecting beautiful "junk."

VARIATIONS

♦ Have your child add to the box by keeping an eye out for beautiful junk.

♦ Have an older child use some of the materials to make a kaleidoscope box for his baby sister or brother. (See the Kaleidoscope activity in the Infants section of this book for details.)

WHAT'S BEING LEARNED

Creativity comes from seeing old stuff in new ways. Assembling miscellaneous objects in a unique way is an effective means of combining both open and focused attention: open attention as children scan their environment and focused attention when they put all the goodies together.

Name the Sounds

Here is a game to play when walking to keep everyone alert to all the sounds around her. This game is so versatile that it can be played with just one other person, with a group of people, or happily all alone. If your child goes on a walk or is playing alone outside, you might ask her to listen to the sounds and tell you about them when she comes in; or, when you are going to be gone for a solitary jog, promise her you'll return and tell her what sounds you heard.

TYPE OF ATTENTION ENCOURAGED

Open

MATERIALS

Paper and pen (optional)

DIRECTIONS

Before you leave the house to walk somewhere, especially if you are going to walk a route you've taken many times and want to excite walkers' attention, ask children to help you guess the number of different sounds you'll hear along the way. Then while walking, say "I can hear a _____" and wait until the others hear that sound too. Keep walking and let everyone have a turn identifying sounds. Writing down each sound makes it easier to remember how many you heard altogether. Did you guess the right number of sounds?

VARIATION

Instead of "I can hear" use "I can see" and point out to each other any interesting thing you spy. You could also be specific about the kinds of things you spy. Only red things? Only things not seen before, such as a new window display, a new kind of car, or a recently bloomed flower? Again, you can guess what number of things you'll see beforehand.

WHAT'S BEING LEARNED

This type of game encourages open attention as it requires continual scanning of the environment with the ears or the eyes.

Navigator

Most children love to look at maps, but can't immediately work out all that they represent in the real world. In this activity, giving your child the responsibility of being a real navigator encourages him to pay attention to what a map is showing.

TYPES OF ATTENTION ENCOURAGED

Open and focused

MATERIALS

Local map of your area

DIRECTIONS

Show your potential navigator how to find where you are on the map. Then show him the place you want to go. Together work out the path you would need to take to get where you want to go.

If this is a brand-new activity for your child, start it by laying out a map on the kitchen table and working out the details together.

Next do the activity in the car with the navigator telling the driver which direction to go to get to your destination: "Take a right on Star Lane," "Now take a left on Coastal Road," and so on.

Start with a simple path that requires only a couple of turns. As your child's skills grow, allow him to navigate more complicated routes.

VARIATION

Once he has the concept, give your child the big assignments on family trips to find the way to the desired destination.

WHAT'S BEING LEARNED

Children are engaging their spatial awareness and using open attention as they get a general overview of your area. Then they are using their focusing skills to work out the specific route to get you where you want to go.

Police Report

Unfortunately, it's all too easy to go about everyday errands and be there only in body, not noticing the details of life. Next time you have to wait in line at the bank or grocery store with your child, try this game to keep both of you focused in the moment.

TYPES OF ATTENTION ENCOURAGED

Open and focused

MATERIALS

None

DIRECTIONS

Pretend that a crime was committed while you were standing there, and you both have to make a witness report to the police or to a newspaper journalist. What was going on around you while you were waiting in line?

For example, if you are in line at the bank, pretend the bank was about to be robbed. Ask your child to look around at the other people who are in line at the bank and to try to remember details about them. What are they wearing? How are they standing? What do you think their attitude is (patiently waiting, fidgety, distracted, and so on)? If there are two people together, guess what their relationship is to each other and maybe even how they are getting along. (Are they friendly, irritated, in love, ignoring each other?) If you overhear a conversation, note the tone and possible feelings of the speakers. Tell your child not to talk about what she's noticed until you're done at the bank.

When you are out of the bank, you and your child report to each other what you saw, thought, and felt. It's fun to see how we all focus in on different details depending on our own unique perspective. Because none of us can really know if our interpretation of what others are feeling is correct, there is no right or wrong in this game, only the enjoyment of watching and guessing.

WHAT'S BEING LEARNED

Children are learning to scan a room using open attention and then focus on particular details that are both emotional and physical. This also helps develop the social skill of reading body language. Having to remember details after the fact also strengthens memory skills.

Ring of String

Often we can look at things without really seeing them. In this game, children are encouraged to look really closely at one spot and to see all there is to see.

TYPE OF ATTENTION ENCOURAGED

Focused

MATERIALS

String
Magnifying glass or jar with water in it (optional)
Tweezer (optional)
Plate (optional)

DIRECTIONS

Make a circle on the ground with the string. The circle can be any size (a 2- to 3-foot circumference works well). Look carefully at the enclosed area with your child and notice what is growing there. Pull out a weed or blade of grass and see what the roots look like. Is there a seedpod in the area? What's inside?

Poke a hole and see if there are any insects around. What are they, and how are they different from each other? What are they doing? Are they scurrying around to hide or curling up and playing dead or not noticing you at all? Is the dirt in the hole you dug any different from the dirt on the ground?

Use a magnifying glass or a jar with water in it and look at various things again. How do they look different now?

Use a tweezer, if handy, to pick up small things to put on a plate so that you can look at them more closely. Things like acorns, petals, seeds, bark, mica, and grains of sand are good to collect and examine.

VARIATION

Pick one area of a garden and notice the types of plants growing there, their similarities and differences, their fragrances and colors.

WHAT'S BEING LEARNED

The ability to be still and look closely at what's near at hand is the attention skill being developed in this game. There is a lot of pleasure to be had from noticing the tiny wonders of nature that are in our own backyard.

Shelf Paper Story

Having a huge roll of paper to draw on without space limitations is almost as good as drawing on a wall and more fun than a pad of paper. In this game, the roll of paper becomes a scroll of your child's life.

TYPES OF ATTENTION ENCOURAGED

Open and focused

MATERIALS

Roll of white shelf paper

Markers, crayons, or colored pencils

DIRECTIONS

Give your child the roll of paper and his drawing materials. Explain that on this paper, he can draw a story about his life. Open the roll of paper and have the child draw a picture of himself on the first section. In the next section he can draw himself doing whatever he did that day or a few of the things that happened that day.

Each day, he can add to the scroll. The paper can be kept rolled up and be added to when the mood strikes.

VARIATION

If he doesn't want to draw his life, any subject is fine, or even just whimsical designs.

WHAT'S BEING LEARNED

Because they have the freedom to express whatever story or art idea they come up with, children are encouraged to use open attention to think about what is possible. Then, no matter what they decide to do, drawing is a good focusing skill.

Thinking Box

It's easy to get distracted while doing homework. The essence of this activity is to make a space that is conducive to those times when concentration and thinking are unavoidable—in other words, when doing that homework.

TYPE OF ATTENTION ENCOURAGED

Focused

MATERIALS

Large box (such as the kind a computer or printer would come in)
Decorative materials, such as photos of favorite characters, bright
(yellow or red) or calming (blue or green) paint, soothing wallpa-
per design
Glue, scissors, tape, and so on
Large clip

DIRECTIONS

Have your child make a Thinking Box by decorating it inside and out in a
way that will make her happy just looking at it. The box should be turned
on its side for decorating.

When it's homework time, place the box on the kitchen table or your
child's desk so that it makes a private hideaway.

Inside the box, have a light, a timer (or clock), and a fresh supply of
pens, pencils, and erasers. Put a clip on the side of the box so that each day
the student can put up a list of the homework she needs to do.

Have your child look at her assignment list and decide how much time she
will need to do each assignment. For
example, she might take twenty minutes
to do math problems and then take a
three-minute break to eat a snack before
going back to work for another ten minutes on more math or another subject. As
each assignment gets done, she checks it
off her list. She can use the timer to help
her stay focused and keep to this schedule.

Oddly enough, limiting one's times
helps expand it. If the time to do her math
homework, for example, is open ended—
"Work at it until it's done"—it can invite
daydreaming and time wasting. If the

child knows she has to concentrate for only a short burst, she'll find the whole process more manageable, one burst at a time.

WHAT'S BEING LEARNED

By creating their own space, children are learning one way to keep their attention focused on one task, such as doing homework. Making a pleasing physical barrier keeps them from being easily distracted. They are also learning how to organize their time by setting their own schedule. And they are learning that you respect their ability to make their own decisions.

- ~ - ~ - ~ - ~ - ~ - ~ - ~ - ~ - ~ - ~ -

I'm the Teacher

Reading is a visual process, which is fine unless you happen to learn better through your ears. In this activity, children who don't always understand what they read get to hear the words spoken. What's even better is that they get to be the all-knowing teacher.

TYPE OF ATTENTION ENCOURAGED

Focused

MATERIALS

Video recorder

DIRECTIONS

Ask your learner to pretend that he is the teacher and is reading to his class. Have him pick some dry material that he is having difficulty understanding. Set up the video recorder so that he can sit (or stand) and read to his class.

Suggest, or model, that he read with style, emphasizing the important points, so that when he watches the tape, he can take notes and learn from his "teacher." Do a few practice runs, if he wants, before you turn on the recorder.

VARIATION

Use a tape recorder.

WHAT'S BEING LEARNED

♦ Pretending to be someone who is more capable has the amazing effect of making children feel and be more capable.

♦ Reading aloud by performing in front of a camera increases children's alertness and attention.

♦ Because another pathway is stimulated, listening to what is being read makes it easier to understand.

♦ Taking notes on what they are hearing puts the material through even a third pathway, the kinesthetic one.

♦ They will understand that material!

My Mind Is a TV Screen

This game is especially good if your child sometimes has difficulty with reading comprehension. It encourages the skill of visualization, which is what makes a book come alive.

TYPE OF ATTENTION ENCOURAGED

Open

MATERIALS

Book (not a picture book)

DIRECTIONS

Before you read a book to your child, tell her that the game is for her to take your words and turn them into a mental picture by visualizing what she hears as a TV show or movie.

Begin by reading a selection. The following is an example: "Jacob was on his favorite merry-go-round in the park. There was a delightful breeze that made his shirt billow. He smiled, enjoying the ride, and thought about the candy he wanted to buy after the ride was done."

To help your child visualize, ask questions about the passage you read. For example:

"What do you think the merry-go-round looks like?"
"What kind of shirt do you see Jacob wearing?"
"What kinds of candy do you imagine he is thinking about?"

Once she gets the idea, read on! If your child appears to be intently listening, don't stop. If she appears to have gotten distracted, stop and talk about the movie you are seeing in your head to help her get back into the scene.

VARIATIONS

♦ Ask her to play the same game after she has silently read to herself, and to tell you details about what she saw as she was reading.

♦ As you read together, ask her to guess what will happen next. Can she predict where the story is heading and imagine the ending or next part?

WHAT'S BEING LEARNED

Children are tapping into the right brain's capacity to visualize. This skill will not only lengthen their attention span but also help them comprehend stories.

Visualizing also encourages imagination, a necessary ingredient in personal entertainment.

If you play the variation of having your child guess what will happen next, you are giving her practice in the important skill of previewing. This is the skill that is necessary when we are planning any project. We need to have a vision of where we are going in order to get there. When we are writing a report, we need to know what the final paragraph will be so that we can keep in mind where we are going as we write. Whether we are sculpting, building a house, or planning a garden, knowing our destination strengthens our navigation.

Paper Plethora

One of the ways to increase a child's attention span is to give him things that encourage his creativity. Paper is an inexpensive medium for exploring because it can be torn, ripped, wadded, crumpled, folded, taped, pasted, rolled, wrapped, and scribbled on.

Over a month's time, squirrel away any interesting paper or cardboard that crosses your path and put the pieces in a special box for this purpose.

TYPES OF ATTENTION ENCOURAGED

Open and focused

MATERIALS

Scraps of different kinds of paper, such as gift wrapping paper, wax paper, discarded envelopes, toothpaste boxes, gift boxes, photocopy paper, colored paper, aluminum foil, magazines, greeting cards, and paper bags

Glue or tape (or both)

Crayons or markers

DIRECTIONS

One morning, especially if it's a rainy, nothing-to-do, "I'm bored" day, announce that it's Paper Day and assign some floor space or a table for the event. Bring out the box of paper goodies and let your child have at them. He'll probably come up with some ideas that are totally his own, or you might suggest some of these:

- Tear out magazine pictures and paste them on a paper to make a collage.

- Crumple up a small piece of paper and cover it with tape, making a small ball. Take turns tossing the ball into the gift box for a game.

- Make new greeting cards out of wrapping paper designs or old greeting cards.

- Make sculptures out of aluminum foil.

- Write pretend letters and put them in envelopes to "mail" to each other.

- Cut lots of types of paper up into teeny pieces to make confetti, then write your child's name on white paper in glue and pour the confetti onto the glue.

WHAT'S BEING LEARNED

Children are learning the magic of imagination and creativity and the way it captures one's attention. They are noticing aspects of old materials and coming up with creative ways to make something different, which encourages their global attentive skills. They are also learning one of those important lifelong skills: how to entertain themselves with whatever is around them.

Potato Puppets

Puppets are always a great way for children to stretch their imagination by focusing on being someone else. We can inspire and excite their imagination by doing this variation on the classic toy, Mr. Potato Head. In this version, you use a real potato!

TYPE OF ATTENTION ENCOURAGED

Focused

MATERIALS

Potatoes

Knife (for adult use only)

Straight pins, thumbtacks, toothpicks, or paper and glue

Red felt-tip marker (optional)

Yarn, handkerchief, or aluminum foil

DIRECTIONS

Take a small potato and cut a hole in one end large enough for one or two fingers to fit into.

For eyes and nose, your child can poke in pieces of paper or other objects with straight pins or thumbtacks, or she can paste on dots of paper.

For the mouth, she can dig out a round hole and color it with red felt-tip marker, draw a mouth on paper and paste it or tack it on, or scratch on a "happy face" smile with a pin.

The hair can be a handkerchief tied around the head, bits of yarn pinned into the top, or torn strips of aluminum foil pinned to the head for the "heavy metal" look.

Once the puppets are made, act out a scenario. It could be the events of that day, starting from that morning, or it could be a pretend situation, such as going to see the doctor or being an actress getting interviewed at the debut of her big Potato Head film.

You can also take advantage of stories already written and act out your version of a classic fairy tale.

VARIATIONS

♦ If you want to use your Halloween pumpkin-carving skills, get as elaborate as you want with mouths that have teeth and eyes that are deep set and have raisins for pupils. You can get as simple or as complex as seems fitting to the moment and age level.

♦ Don't have a potato handy? You can also do simple instant puppets by wrapping an adhesive bandage around your sweetie's finger and drawing a face on it.

◆ Puppets can also be made out of
small paper bags. This is good if you and
yours are in a crayoning mood and want
to draw the puppet's facial details.

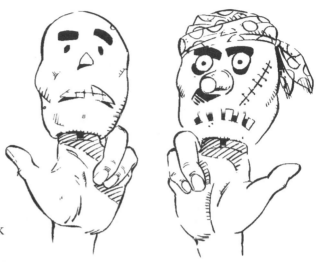

WHAT'S BEING LEARNED

Children are learning to focus their
attention by concentrating on decorating the potato.

Their creativity is also being stimulated
when they choose how their potato will look
and how they will act in the play.

Sensory Matching

*Paying attention to the world means noticing details and seeing patterns in
things. To help encourage this awareness, we can teach children to notice
the many ways things are similar and different from each other. In this
game, objects are distinguished by texture and smell, but there are many
other ways that kids can be encouraged to notice details.*

*Because this game takes a bit of preparation, your child can gain dou-
bly from it by helping you prepare.*

TYPES OF ATTENTION ENCOURAGED

Open and focused

MATERIALS

Common household items or fabrics of different textures (see individual activities)
Index cards, heavy paper, or light cardboard

DIRECTIONS

Texture Matching

Gather up pairs of lightweight objects, such as cotton balls, pieces of wax paper, pieces of sandpaper, macaroni noodles, pieces of cellophane, rubber bands, pieces of sponge, scraps of fabric, pennies, straws, and so on. Or you might want to use just different textures of fabrics instead of household objects.

Glue each item on a index card so that you end up with two identical sets of cards.

Place one set of cards in front of the player. You keep the other set. Blindfold the player or have her put her hands behind her back; have her feel one card. "Which card on the table is the same as the one you are feeling? Is it card number 1, card number 2, or card number 3?"

If the child is having difficulty, make sure that the differences are not subtle at first; for example, have her distinguish between a cotton ball and a piece of macaroni, or between a piece of sandpaper and a piece of velvet. It's even okay if she needs a "teeny peek." This is a game, after all.

If the child guesses correctly, give her a joyous high five and up the challenge by being increasingly subtle—now comparing a penny and a dime or corduroy and denim, for example.

Smell Matching

Make scratch-and-sniff cards by first mixing a scent, such as cinnamon, cloves, perfume, vanilla or other extract, garlic powder, pencil shavings, soap, or essential oils, with a texture, such as sand, salt, or glitter. Paint some glue on a card and pour on the scented texture. Make two cards of each scent so that you have two sets. Let the cards dry, and shake off the excess.

Have the players rub or scratch each of the cards and find the card with the matching scent.

VARIATION

Have children feel and identify letters and numbers. You can use plastic refrigerator magnets or make letters and numbers with glue on a piece of paper. When the glue dries, it pops up a little, giving the players something to feel.

WHAT'S BEING LEARNED

Children are expanding their discriminatory tactile and olfactory skills and forming connections between how things feel and smell and how they look.

Tile Painting

When we are sculpting something out of sand at the beach, we are unlikely to feel very critical of our efforts. We know that in a short time the ocean will erase it all, and we can just enjoy the process.

If we are feeling insecure about our artistic ability, a piece of paper can be intimidating because the results are permanent. When we look at our work with too critical an eye, it deflates us and takes all the fun out of the artistic process.

Painting or drawing on tiles, an instantly erasable medium, gives children the opportunity to focus on drawing or doodling without the fear of permanence. The smoothness of the tile's surface invites ease in drawing, and the tissue immediately wipes away the last drawing and readies the tile for the next. Children can experience only the best part of creativity: the creating.

TYPE OF ATTENTION ENCOURAGED

Focused

MATERIALS

Plain white or lightly colored glazed tiles, any size
Colored felt-tip pens or paints

DIRECTIONS

Encourage your child to draw or paint on a blank tile using colored pens or paints. He can create an instant image and then when done, wipe it off with a damp paper towel and do another and another. Or he can work on one image and use the corner of the towel or a cotton-tipped swab to wipe away any part that doesn't please him, and redo it.

VARIATIONS

Have several tiles available, so your child can do many versions and later decide which, if any, he wants to save.

   If he does want to save it, take a picture, make a copy on a color copier, or cover the tile with clear cellophane tape or clear contact paper.

WHAT'S BEING LEARNED

By starting with a nonintimidating way to make art, children may find out that it is an enjoyable way to gather their energy and focus. If it turns out that this form of expression is right for them, they may end up carrying around a sketchbook, painting on canvases, or designing a wall mural. Who knows!

Backwards Time Management

Learning time management does not sound like a fun activity, but in this game, your child will learn how to organize her time in an enjoyable way, by thinking backwards.

TYPE OF ATTENTION ENCOURAGED

   Focused

MATERIALS

   Paper and pen
   Digital camera and printer (optional)

DIRECTIONS

Help your child organize her morning by planning it backwards. Start with what time she has to be in school. Have her write "Get to school" and the time at the top of the page. She figures out how long it takes to get to school and what time she would like to start in order to arrive on time. Have her write that event and time down next. Then she figures how long she would like to spend eating breakfast, subtracting that time from the time she needs to leave by, and writing that time next on the list. Ask her to keep working backwards until she gets to what time she has to wake up.

She gets to decide how long she would like each part to take, and fills in the chart.

To make the chart more cheerful, take digital photos of her eating, brushing her teeth, and so on and have her paste each picture beside the appropriate time on the chart.

VARIATION

Instead of using photos, your child can draw appropriate pictures beside each time.

WHAT'S BEING LEARNED

Children are learning to manage their time, which is a vital skill that requires constant attention. This backwards charting is a fun way to get the hang of considering all aspects of scheduling. If children get in the time management habit early on, it will serve them all their life.

Toe Stepping

Here's a fun and silly game that requires concentration and quick movement. Try it at a birthday party gathering when you want to redirect excess energy or when the kids are bored and want something quick and new to do.

TYPE OF ATTENTION ENCOURAGED

Focused

MATERIALS

None

DIRECTIONS

Two people, both barefoot or in stocking feet, face each other and hold hands. Each person tries to step on the other's toes while at the same time keeping his toes from being stepped on.

You might remind the players to step lightly on each other's toes so that others will do the same to them. In other words, follow this game's Golden Rule: step on others as you would want to be stepped on.

VARIATION

Both players, while sitting, put their hands flat on the table, palms down. Each player tries to lightly tap the top of the other player's hand while at the same time keeping his own hands from getting tapped.

WHAT'S BEING LEARNED

Concentrating on both keeping out of the way and going for the goal is a kind of trial by fire. Pressure on their foot lets them know when they weren't paying close enough attention!

Toothpick Art

Some children have a hard time writing legibly or fast enough to get their assignments down. Often the problem is not in the head but in the hands. They just don't have good fine motor control.

There are many ways to teach the hands to be less clumsy and to have more finesse. This is one of them that you can do together.

TYPES OF ATTENTION ENCOURAGED

Open and focused

MATERIALS

Toothpicks, plain or colored

DIRECTIONS

Make an abstract design by laying toothpicks out on a table or floor, with each player adding her toothpick to the design. The first player puts down one toothpick and the next adds hers at just the angle that seems pleasing to her. The next person then adds a toothpick to that design, and so on and so on until an interesting design is formed.

VARIATION

Make a specific scene—for example, a house with a picket fence and trees. Each of you can work on different parts of the scene.

WHAT'S BEING LEARNED

It takes concentration to pick up a skinny toothpick and decide on the best place to put it. Placing each toothpick down carefully and trying not to jiggle the design encourage awareness of hand movements.

This activity also develops the pincer grasp, which uses the small muscles that control the index finger and thumb.

If the design gets mildly jiggled, let your child repair it as part of the learning experience if she wants to. If the design gets hopelessly jumbled because of excess movement, have an easygoing attitude ("Guess that one is done and it's time to start a new one!") so that learning to be okay with mistakes is part of the game.

- ~ - ~ - ~ - ~

PART FIVE

Games for Teens

The games in this part of the book center around ways to help teenagers stay focused by attending to the present moment. When older children are feeling anxious and uncomfortable, they, as we all do, mentally leave the present moment and go to the past or the future in their minds. What we want to teach them is that they can stay engaged in the present, even if it's not a happy moment, because the time will pass. They don't have to like, relish, or enjoy every moment; they just need to acknowledge that this is the kind of moment they are having and go on.

These games help the players be more comfortable with what is happening because they give them ways to deal with difficulties and develop a positive attitude. When teens are confident in their life skills, they find it easier to stay focused and present.

Accentuate the Positive

Being involved in the social scene at school can be a very distracting experience. It's hard to concentrate on lessons when one is thinking of a recent cutting remark or feeling a fear of rejection.

In this game, teens are encouraged to shift their attention and notice positive attributes of the people around them and how these people enrich their lives.

MATERIALS

Paper and pen

DIRECTIONS

Suggest to your teen that she make a list of the people in her life and write down beside each name a positive aspect of having that person in her life. She may find it hard to think of the positives for some people, so maybe it's that they teach her a difficult lesson.

Here are some examples:

Joan: Helps me think more clearly because of her ability to analyze situations.

Lorraine: Makes me look closely at my actions because she is likely to question them.

Don: Makes me feel good about myself because he adores me.

Patty: Makes me more interested in doing physical things because she fills her life with physical activities.

WHAT'S BEING LEARNED

Teens are learning that everyone has a place in their lives and that even difficult friends can be useful.

Negative thinking brings up negative feelings, whereas positive thoughts can have a soothing effect. This game can help teens return to an easier state of mind, and in that state it is easier to concentrate on the task at hand.

Achy Breaky Heart

There's no way around it. Life gives everyone some very sad and difficult moments. Whether the moments are small rejections or bouts of intense grief, a broken heart distracts our ability to focus. Here is one activity for dealing with hurt that my friends Cindy, Robin, and Shirley did as part of their work with hospice. (Hospice helps the terminally ill and their families cope with death and the dying process.)

My friends ran a weekly group with children who had experienced the death of someone they loved. One of the activities that the children really responded to well was Achy Breaky Heart.

TYPES OF ATTENTION ENCOURAGED

Open and focused

MATERIALS

Paper and pen
Tape
Colored pens (optional)

DIRECTIONS

Have your teen draw a large heart on a piece of paper and cut it out. On one side of the heart, he should write down all the difficult things, big and little, that happened that broke his heart. He could also color in the heart or draw designs on it. Next, he should tear up the heart into small pieces.

Next have him take the small pieces and, as though putting together a puzzle, make the heart whole again and tape it back together. Put the tape on the side of the heart where the words are written.

On the other side of the mended heart, your teen writes down all the things he did to feel good again, such as being with friends, doing some kind of artwork, listening to music, riding a horse, swimming, and so on.

VARIATION

Suggest that he write a story about a character who had this difficult experience and all the things he did that helped him heal.

WHAT'S BEING LEARNED

Even though there is something to be said for the comfortableness of denial, often there is no other way of dealing with difficulty than facing it directly. This activity helps young people acknowledge their pain and notice the methods they used to recover. It offers them the comfort of knowing that they can bring themselves their own relief.

Suppressed painful feelings can take the form of hyperactivity, which becomes a method of avoiding the feelings that will come to the surface with stillness. Recognizing and reducing discomfort by realizing that they are able to handle pain enhances adolescents' ability to concentrate even when they are going through difficult times.

Annoyed with the Flower Bud

Sometimes I find I get annoyed with myself because I'm not further along with something. Sometimes it's my spiritual practice: I wish I'd remember to stay present more often. Or it's my career: I wish I would be consistently better at what I do. Or it's a relationship. We all have times when we get impatient with our progress.

When I'm in that kind of mood or when I'm with teenagers who feel discouraged about their progress, this game helps.

TYPES OF ATTENTION ENCOURAGED

Open and focused

MATERIALS

None

DIRECTIONS

Go up to a flowering bush with your adolescent and notice together the various stages of flower development on one plant: the bud, the young flower unfurling, the flower in full bloom, the bloom starting to wilt, the flower with small seeds forming inside.

Ask your companion if it makes her want to yell at the bud and say, "Hurry up, bud, move along! Why aren't you in full bloom yet? Look at this other flower; it's way ahead of you. What's holding you back? You're just wasting your time being a bud when you're supposed to be a blooming flower. Get on with it!"

More likely you'd think, "How fragile and beautiful you are just as you are. Relax and take your time. You can't help but bloom someday and then you'll age and make seeds for others." Encourage your young bud to think about the flowers when she feels that she's not getting somewhere fast enough.

The thought of pushing the flower bud to be more than it is seems ridiculous, and as part of nature, we need to see that we are also growing in different aspects of our lives at our own pace. We are opening and growing little by little and day by day.

VARIATION

Give your child other examples of things growing at their own pace. For example, one would not criticize a toddler who is just learning to walk as being inadequate when he falls down, or critique the new artwork of a beginning artist because it was not up to the quality of an experienced artist.

WHAT'S BEING LEARNED

Teens are learning to accept that everything happens in its time. Just as yelling at a flower bud or tugging at the grass won't make it grow faster, being impatient with the speed of one's learning and growing won't make things happen any faster.

They are also learning to look to nature for patterns that also apply to human nature. This encourages a more global and open attentive approach to life. Also, by noticing nature's small details, they are developing their concentrated focusing skills.

Five Good Moments

A friend and I were eagerly looking forward to seeing each other at the end of the day, but didn't want to wish the day away in our anticipation. So we made a plan that when we got together we would tell each other five good things that happened that day. Instead of wishing the day would hurry up and be over, we paid close attention to what was happening so that we would have good stories to recount.

You can encourage your teen to play this game with you to help him develop an attentive eye toward his day that's focused on the positive.

TYPES OF ATTENTION ENCOURAGED

Open and focused

MATERIALS

None

DIRECTIONS

Suggest to your teen, "Pay attention throughout the day for five moments that make you feel good. The moment can be an interaction with someone or a thought inspired by something that happened or a sight or a sound that you thought lovely. What it is doesn't matter. What matters is that for at least a moment it made you feel good. I'll do the same. When we get together at the end of the day, we'll share our five good things that happened."

VARIATIONS

- High-Low. Instead of noticing five good things, notice both the high of the day and the low.

- My Story. Ask your teen to write down one of the things that happened as a short story or vignette. Make a small book and add stories to it over the years as a kind of autobiography that your child might someday share with his own children or leaf through when he is older.

WHAT'S BEING LEARNED

Teens are learning to pay attention to all the events that happen in a day and then focus in on the positive aspects by intentionally looking for them.

This game also encourages players to pay attention to how specific events make them feel.

This activity is a reminder that life contains many kinds of moments. Often teens get stuck on a negative moment and enlarge its significance, such as when they hear a criticism and believe that it means they are hopelessly hopeless. This game shows young people that good moments are always part of the mix if they keep a lookout for them.

Getting the Priorities

I heard this story about a professor who was trying to teach his students a life lesson. He took a clear, narrow-necked vase and filled it with as many large stones as could fit through the neck. Then he asked his students if the vase was full. They said it was. "Wrong," he said, and then filled it with small pebbles that he shook down until he got in all he could. "Full now?" he asked. "Yes," they said. "Wrong," he countered, and proceeded to fill up every nook and cranny with fine sand. "Now?" he asked. "Absolutely!" they replied. Then he poured in some water.

"What's the life lesson?" he queried.

"That no matter how full your life seems, there is always room for more," a student ventured.

"Completely the opposite," the professor explained. *"The rocks are the important things in life, such as your health, family, friends, work, spirituality, and community. If I had filled the vase with the other things—the water, the pebbles, and the sand—then the vase would have been full and there would be no room for the rocks."*

The lesson: don't fill up your life with other things until you have made a space for what matters most.

TYPES OF ATTENTION ENCOURAGED

Open and focused

MATERIALS

Paper and pen

DIRECTIONS

To be sure you and your teen have your "rocks" in place, each of you makes a separate list of what matters most to you. Then, under each of these headings, list the things you do that give time and attention to each priority.

If either of you finds that your attention list is more paltry than you would like, list the kinds of things that you could do to enlarge your attention to each heading item.

Here are some examples:

♦ Priority: My little sister

What we do now: eat dinner together, sometimes read her stories before bed, watch television, take a two-week vacation together with the family to visit Grandma.

Want to add: walk to the park together more often, play catch, make dates to go ice skating in winter and canoeing on the local lake in summer. Sometimes plan a special date when just the two of us cook dinner for the family or make a special dessert.

♦ Priority: Exercise

What I do now: go to required weekly gym class at school. Walk in the mall with friends.

Want to add: do a Wednesday evening walk with my mom for a half hour, explore and join a fun movement class with my best friend (circuit training to music, tango lesson, yoga for teens, or whatever sounds doable for us)

VARIATION

Do this activity in a group so that everyone can brainstorm ideas to help each other get their priorities met.

WHAT'S BEING LEARNED

Young people can feel distracted, anxious, and unable to focus when they aren't addressing some basic needs, especially if they don't realize that this is what has happened.

In this exercise, we encourage teens to focus on what they need and then open themselves to possible ways to attend to those needs.

This is a lesson that will be useful all their lives.

My Special Things

Teenagers often have some special objects in their room—a stuffed animal that means a lot, a piece of jewelry someone gave them, a rock they found on a meaningful outing. Here is an opportunity to make those objects immortal.

TYPES OF ATTENTION ENCOURAGED

Open and focused

MATERIALS

Paper and pen or computer and word processor
Camera (optional)
Scrapbook

DIRECTIONS

Suggest to your budding writer that she take photographs of the objects in her life that have meaning to her and paste them in a scrapbook. Under each picture, she should write a story about how that object came into her life and what it means to her.

VARIATION

Instead of taking a picture, she could draw the object.

WHAT'S BEING LEARNED

This activity is especially good for teens who avoid writing. Because the subject matter is so dear to their hearts, they are more likely to feel inspired to write and, if the variation is used, draw. Personal stories often encourage prolonged attention because the subject is so interesting!

I'm Like That Sometimes

We're told as children that sticks and stones can break our bones but names will never hurt us. But it's not true. Our bones can heal and never bother us again, but a disparaging remark can hurt for a lifetime.

If parents in a frustrating moment hurl a negative character label at their child (for example, telling him he is "mean"), that child, in his impressionable and vulnerable state, can take in that label and deeply believe it. After all, he has had mean thoughts. He may think that the omniscient grown-up knows his secret true self.

It's so uncomfortable to feel bad about oneself that a common way to deal with these kinds of appraisals is to deny them totally. I am not mean!!

The reality is that we all have mean thoughts or say hurtful things sometimes.

In this game, you can help your adolescent cut himself a little slack and see that we are all a mix of all human emotions.

MATERIALS

None

DIRECTIONS

Teach your teen to use the phrase "I'm like that sometimes" if he commits a thoughtless act. Using that expression (or something similar, such as "Sometimes we humans do thoughtless things") makes the act bearable. The attitude is not condemning because the teen is noticing the nature of being human: sometimes we do thoughtless things. By noticing our thoughtless acts we are less likely to commit them again.

VARIATION

Consider sharing some of your own foibles and how you accepted them and learned from them.

WHAT'S BEING LEARNED

We can't fix something if we don't know it's broken. We can't be apologetic or do things a different way if we are vehemently denying that we were in the wrong.

This game helps teenagers be more comfortable with making errors so that they can more easily focus on what needs to be done next or at least the next time. When we turn down the volume of denial, we all can see how it feels better inside to do the thoughtful thing.

"I'm like that sometimes" helps teenagers (and all of us) focus on and be okay with the behavior that could use some adjusting.

Imagine That!

Even though I often come up with ideas for games while taking a long walk, I rarely remember to bring paper and pen with me. I used to have to repeat the ideas to myself several times during the walk to help me remember them. When other thoughts or a spot of nature's beauty would capture my attention, I forgot what my ideas were.

Then I tried a method I had heard about for years to help remember things. The trick is to take all the information you want to remember and form it into a visual image. My friend who taught me the trick could remember as many as fifty things this way. I figured I should be able to use this method to remember four!

So one day when I wanted to remember four of the games for this book—one with a deck of cards, one about writing on backs, one about self-calming techniques, and this visual memory game—I conjured up a picture of a deck of cards calming itself in a hammock while someone was touching its back saying, "Imagine that!"

The technique worked so well that even though I forgot to write the ideas down the minute I got home, I still remembered the image the next morning (even after a full night's set of dreams) and wrote the ideas down.

Try this same technique with your teenager to help her focus on some things she has to remember.

TYPES OF ATTENTION ENCOURAGED

Open and focused

MATERIALS

None

DIRECTIONS

Take any facts your teenager needs to remember, such as facts that need to be memorized for school, and help her make a visual picture that incorporates the key words. The vision doesn't have to make sense and probably works best the more ridiculous it is.

You can practice this technique by taking a grocery list and making a picture in your head that includes all the items. It might look like a pineapple with a sausage link necklace riding on a loaf of bread and . . . well, you get the idea. Go to the store together and see how many items you both remembered using this technique.

VARIATIONS

♦ Make an acronym: use the first letters of each of the items to make a word.

♦ Make an acrostic: use the first letters of the key words to make a sentence.

WHAT'S BEING LEARNED

All children can benefit from incorporating this technique, especially in a school setting. They are learning the benefits of combining focusing with an open imagination. Children with ADD and some children with an Autistic Spectrum Disorder such as Asperger's are said to have superior visual skills and would find it especially helpful.

Send Joy to Bulgaria

Even though feelings of being alone and isolated seem to be part of our human existence, in many ways we are connected to everyone else in the universe. Whatever happens to one of us has an impact on us all.

This game uses that universal connection to help your teenager focus and enjoy trying to connect with someone far away.

TYPE OF ATTENTION ENCOURAGED

Focused

MATERIALS

None

DIRECTIONS

Suggest that you and your adolescent spend a few spare minutes a day, whether sitting on a meditation cushion or waiting for a stoplight to change, sending good thoughts to a stranger in Bulgaria. I chose Bulgaria because I don't know anything about it. I have no preconceived ideas about the politics there or the state of the economy. All I know is that it's very far from where I am and that there is a person there who would benefit from more joy in his or her life. Pick any country you want; there is always someone somewhere who can use a little more joy.

When thinking about that person—and make it the same person each time—imagine that he or she is suddenly feeling happy for no particular reason, simply because he or she was sent a dose of joy from you. Wish for a brighter smile, a lilt in the walk, and a sense of well-being. Imagine that person suddenly stopping and noticed something beautiful—a cloud, a passing butterfly, the graceful form of a tree branch. Imagine this person suddenly filled with an appreciation for life just as it is right now.

Have your child try to imagine details about the person he's chosen. In my imagination, I have picked a farmer. He's of medium height, a little on the skinny side, and graying at his temples. I enjoy sending him little bits of happiness and get pleasure from imagining him surprised by this sudden good feeling inside him. This feeling makes him go kiss his wife, who later happily hums while making yummy biscuits with their children.

Your teen may be surprised at how good it feels to send joy to a complete stranger.

Who knows? Maybe someday I'll actually go to Bulgaria and meet a farmer who finds himself feeling oddly grateful to me but can't imagine why.

VARIATION

Do this for someone you know, but don't necessarily ever tell him or her!

WHAT'S BEING LEARNED

Teens are focusing their attention for brief but intense periods of time and noticing that when they have very uplifting thoughts for someone else, it brings them up too.

Life Is a Movie, and You Are the Star!

Shakespeare said that all the world is a stage and we are the players. That's a useful attitude to take sometimes, because it gives us a more distanced view of our life and helps us avoid getting bogged down in the details.

In this version, all the world is a movie, and we not only have the starring role but also are the directors.

TYPES OF ATTENTION ENCOURAGED

Open and focused

MATERIALS

None or paper and pen

DIRECTIONS

When your teen is in a challenging situation, have her imagine that she is the director and the star in a movie scene. What is the general theme of this movie? What scene is she in? Who are the supporting players? What are the main characters doing? What are they learning? What ideally happens next?

For example, the movie is about a young woman's life and how she finds ways to maintain a positive view of herself and survive in a difficult situation.

The scene is of her boyfriend telling her that he wants to break up with her to be with someone else.

The main characters could be the young woman, her boyfriend, her consoling best friend, and the "other woman."

As the star, your teen will feel the emotions that the main character is going through—the sadness, the anger, the sense of being abandoned and rejected.

As the director, she can have great sympathy for the heroine and want the audience to feel her plight. Being the maker of many tales, however, she also knows that there is growth in even the most dire circumstances, and she starts planning the scenes that will show the audience how the heroine is able to move on and go forward.

Have your teen sketch out, in her mind or on paper, a storyboard of different possible scenes that could follow the break-up scene (including time for the heroine to experience her appropriate sad feelings).

VARIATION

Act the parts out! Your director-screenwriter can play all the parts or give out parts for others to do.

WHAT'S BEING LEARNED

By seeing their experience from a wider perspective, teens can both have compassion for themselves and come to accept their situation as just a part of life, like a scene in a movie. They can also influence the next, more positive scene through their focused intention.

This game also helps give teens a sense of connection with the human dilemma and the experiences we all have in common. The feeling of abandonment, for example, can come in different story lines, but we all know it. If we don't accept the naturalness of our feelings in this situation, we might spend our time thinking, "How could he leave me? There must be something wrong with me." When we take that route, we can't begin to notice anything else around us; we're too busy spiraling down in our thoughts. If instead we were to say to ourselves something like, "Ouch—that hurt. No wonder I feel bad. I wonder what will happen next?" we are going to be more able to deal with *what is*. Developing this kind of acceptance makes it easier to deal with what is and stay attentive to what is happening.

List Your Options

Teens often act impulsively. They respond to something without thinking instead of taking the time to review their options and choose the most effective response.

In this game, adolescents get the experience of seeing their options before and even after the fact. Seeing one's options is helpful in preparing for possibilities and also in learning from mistakes.

TYPE OF ATTENTION ENCOURAGED

Open

MATERIALS

Paper and pen
Index cards (optional)

DIRECTIONS

Make up scenarios or use ones that have happened. With your teenager, list on paper or index cards all the possible ways to respond to the situation.

List all options, even if they seem silly or mean. The idea is to list as many options as you can think of.

Example: A classmate cut in front of you at the drinking fountain. What are your options?

1. Shove the kid away and get your place back.
2. Tell the teacher.
3. Say nothing but plan revenge.
4. Say something like "Hey, that's my spot. Move to the back."
5. Wonder why this person feels the need to be first.

6. Say something to him later, such as "It ticked me off when you pushed ahead of me. Don't do that again."

7. Say something loudly in line about this person shoving ahead, especially to the people behind you who were also affected, such as "Why does this guy think he has the right to push ahead of us??"

8. Say derogatory things about this person to others in private.

9. Paste notices around the school that say, "Joshua cuts in line."

10. Make a pass at his girlfriend.

Beside each option, write down the possible consequences. Comment on the pros and cons of each. Discuss which ones feel comfortable, which might be most effective in that situation, and which ones could be practiced and learned.

VARIATIONS

♦ Look at the options in a "big picture" situation. For example, what options did a leader of a country have at a critical period of history? What were other options for George W. Bush besides going to war with Iraq? What were other options for Rosa Parks besides refusing to give up her seat on the bus?

♦ Look at the options in a smaller picture, such as a situation on a television show. What options did Homer Simpson have in the last episode you saw of *The Simpsons?*

WHAT'S BEING LEARNED

When teenagers can see all the choices they have, they can significantly lighten the load of the problem and enlarge their global attentive skills. Some of their suggested responses are sure to elicit giggles and perhaps the mental satisfaction of revenge without the messy consequences.

Young people also get a chance to really look at the consequences of each option and see which outcomes they would prefer. Having this open awareness will help them develop impulse control and guide them in choosing other options the next time.

If the variations are played, teenagers gain the awareness that all humans have to make choices and all these choices lead to consequences, which in turn lead to the possibility of different choices. We're all learning.

Name the Consequences

When teenagers are afraid of a situation, one way for them to stay focused in the moment is to look squarely at the possible consequences and make alternative plans for dealing with them. When teenagers worry that something is not going to go the way they hoped, suggest that instead of panicking, they make a list!

Once they see clearly that they can handle various possible consequences, adolescents often can relax and deal with what is happening.

TYPES OF ATTENTION ENCOURAGED

Open and focused

MATERIALS

Paper and pen

DIRECTIONS

When your child is afraid of a situation, such as a big test or a new experience, suggest she make a list of what is scaring her. Start with the fear and then break it down into its separate components. Under each component, write the possible solutions that will help. Under that, write how she will deal with that component even if all solutions fail! The following is an example.

Fear: I'm afraid of going on this trip to a foreign country.

♦ Fear 1: The plane ride is so long. I'm afraid of being bored or antsy.

Possible solutions: Bring a book I've already started and am involved in, the sewing project I want to finish, a computer, digital music, video game player, or anything that is engrossing.

If all else fails: Remember that the plane ride will end, and it's only a few hours in my life.

♦ Fear 2: I don't speak the language, and I'll get lost.

Possible solutions: Bring a dictionary and write out and practice key phrases ahead of time, such as "Hello," "Good-bye," and "Where is the bathroom?" Have the hotel or host write out the address of where you are staying in the local language so that you can show it to cab drivers or others.

If all else fails: Remember the kindness of strangers.

♦ Fear 3: I'll miss my family and friends and be lonely.

Possible solutions: Bring Internet addresses and phone numbers. Modify my perspective so that instead of loneliness, I'll appreciate solitude or being an interested observer. Sit in the park or at a café and watch others. Go to a museum and enjoy the fact that I can see whatever exhibits interest me without considering others' needs. Be open to making a new friend. Write about my feelings in a journal.

If all else fails: Remember that no one dies from short-term loneliness.

♦ Fear 4: I'll hate it and want to go home.

Possible solutions: Take a short trip to somewhere else that I may like better. Get a calendar to mark off the days I have left, but on each day write down something good that happened.

If all else fails: Go home. Set aside extra money for this in case there is a fee for changing the ticket.

VARIATIONS

This activity is intrinsically variable!

WHAT'S BEING LEARNED

Teenagers are learning that they can deal with what happens by being open to alternatives and focusing on solutions. Having the solution ready in advance allows them to pay attention to what is actually happening.

Postcard Diaries

Next time you take a trip with your teenage child, buy him postcards that he can use to make a memorable diary.

TYPES OF ATTENTION ENCOURAGED

Open and focused

MATERIALS

Postcards
Pen
Stamps (optional)
Ribbon or key chain (optional)

DIRECTIONS

Let your teenager select a few postcards each day or at each destination during your trip. As he writes entries on the back of each postcard, he is making a diary for that period of his life.

He can either mail the postcards home to himself or make a hole in one corner of each postcard and string them together with a ribbon or key chain.

VARIATIONS

You don't need to leave home to do this activity. Find postcards that depict various places in your town or get some from a local museum.

If you go to a museum, go to the gift shop first and buy postcards that show items in the museum's collection. Have your teenager look for each item as you tour the museum. Then he can use the cards to write about what the item made him feel or think, or just about his trip to the museum in general.

He can also make puzzles (and keep his words very private) by cutting up a postcard into smaller pieces, which he can put together later.

WHAT'S BEING LEARNED

Teenagers will be learning to scan the environment, both internal and external, to focus in on special things and feelings to put in their postcard diary.

In the museum variation, teenagers are encouraged to scan their surroundings in order to locate the item on the postcard, then to focus in on detail in describing their feelings and experiences.

Scriptwriter

It's hard to stay in the present moment. Our minds are always trying to distract us, going over something that happened before or urging us to imagine something that might (or might not) happen later on.

Pretending to be a scriptwriter and thinking about the different aspects of a scene is a good trick for staying alert to what is happening now.

TYPE OF ATTENTION ENCOURAGED

Focused

MATERIALS

None

DIRECTIONS

Show your teenager how to be a scriptwriter by describing the action. For example, if she's washing dishes, the script might sound like this:

"She's running the hot water, and it feels pleasant on her hands. She pours in some detergent and swishes it around, making the bubbles multiply. She reaches for the blue cup, noticing the familiar cornflower design as she slips it into the water. Behind her she hears the radio from the other room playing a popular tune, and her younger sisters arguing. She reaches for the plate; the smell of the lasagna still lingers on it [and so on and so on]."

VARIATION

Instead of speaking the commentary, sing it.

WHAT'S BEING LEARNED

There are so many aspects to each moment if we just pay attention! Scriptwriting is another way to increase teenagers' awareness of the many details of their lives.

Self-Portraits

Many teenagers go through a phase when they become fascinated with their reflection in the mirror, especially during the period when their faces make that change from a child's to a young adult's.

In this activity, you and your changing child can take advantage of this fascination by drawing your mirror reflections.

TYPE OF ATTENTION ENCOURAGED

Focused

MATERIALS

Mirror
Paper and pencil

DIRECTIONS

Both of you sit facing a mirror and draw yourselves. Try to draw faithfully exactly what you see.

VARIATIONS

♦ Draw each other's reflections.

♦ Look only at your reflection but not at the paper until you are done. This often gives a kind of Picasso look to the work.

WHAT'S BEING LEARNED

Staring at one's face while trying to draw it exactly can be riveting. Concentrating on being very exact can overpower any negative judging voice and enhance your adolescent's focusing skills.

Ten Breaths

Being aware of one's breathing is an ancient technique for pulling in scattered energy and consciously focusing it.

In this game you can show your teenager how to take advantage of this simple technique by playing it whenever she needs to center herself and regroup.

TYPES OF ATTENTION ENCOURAGED

Open and focused

MATERIALS

None

DIRECTIONS

Have your teen start by telling herself that she intends to pay attention to her breathing for the next ten breaths.

As she notices the first inhalation, she should say in her mind, "I'm breathing in one." When her body exhales, she should say, "I'm breathing out one." At the next inhalation she says "I'm breathing in two," and when her body exhales, says "I'm breathing out two," and so on.

This is different from purposely breathing in and out ten times. In this game, she should just be watching her body breathe and naming each breath.

She'll probably notice that different breaths will have different rhythms. Sometimes one breath will follow another at a regular interval; other times, there might be a long gap between breaths. Some breaths are shallow, others deep. The idea is just to notice and name the number.

She'll probably find, as most people do, that this task is easier said than done. We tend to get distracted by passing thoughts, and we may get only to "I'm breathing in three" before we go on a little mind trip. That's okay. When this happens, she can smile at herself and her mind excursion. Suggest that instead of being harsh, she be exuberant that she noticed and is now back. (I like to say, "I'm back!" in a congratulatory tone.) Then she can go back to the beginning: "I'm breathing in one."

The fun and challenging part of this game is for her to see how far she can get before she "leaves." Some days may be a "five day" because she can't seem to get past the fifth breath before she forgets what she was doing. Other days, she might find it so easy to focus that she decides to go on to fifteen or more breaths.

VARIATIONS

♦ Suggest that while she is waiting for her body to breath in or out, she stay in control of her mind by using that millisecond to notice what her senses are experiencing. Hear the sounds. Feel the temperature. Notice the air movements. Bringing in sensory awareness will give her the feeling that she is very much in the scene and not separate from it.

♦ Instead of breaths, count steps. If your teen is feeling too anxious to sit still but wants to get in a centered mental state, suggest that she take a small walk and count each step. Suggest that she be aware of the sensations her feet are having as they push off from the ground with each forward step. Focusing and concentrating on her steps is calming because it helps her stay present with the walking experience.

WHAT'S BEING LEARNED

Teens are practicing focusing their attention deliberately so that they are consciously aware of being present in each moment. These short bursts of deliberate focusing have a cumulative affect. The more experience teenagers have, the more familiar that state of mind becomes and the easier it is to return to.

If they do the first variation, they are also experiencing being fluid between focused and open attention. They are focusing their attention on the breath, and in between breaths they are scanning the environment for sensory information.

This game also helps teens become aware of how easy it is to get distracted, and they gain a sense of the level of awareness that is needed to get back on track.

The Home Videographer

We don't have to see reality shows only on television; we can make our own. In this activity, your teen gets the opportunity to make a family archive for posterity.

TYPES OF ATTENTION ENCOURAGED

Open and focused

MATERIALS

Video camera

DIRECTIONS

First have family members agree to having a film made of their lives.

Then encourage your filmmaker to take footage of scenes from daily family life—for example, Mom doing her Pilates exercise, Dad making his famous French toast, Sister yakking on the phone, Grandma at a protest rally, the pet dog and cat nuzzling.

VARIATION

We can turn the tables in this activity by joining in and getting behind the camera for a look at the videographer at home. Take shots of him going about his daily business, including real things like arguing with his siblings. Getting objective feedback on how we are in the world can help us make needed changes. Seeing ourselves on camera can give us some clear insight into how we are—the good and the bad—or, at least, encourage us to laugh at ourselves.

WHAT'S BEING LEARNED

Teenagers are getting experience in opening and being aware of all that is happening around them and then focusing in on particulars.

Waiter, Take My Order

When you go to a restaurant and place an order with a waitperson, you don't sit around wondering if your order will be filled. You might get impatient if it takes longer than you want, but you don't doubt that your food will come.

This same hopefulness and expectation can serve us and our children in a larger realm. Sometimes in order for our intentions to be fulfilled, we have to expect that they will be.

In this game, you and your teen place your orders for your life.

TYPES OF ATTENTION ENCOURAGED

Open and focused

MATERIALS

None or paper and pen

DIRECTIONS

Pretend that you and your teenager are at the restaurant of life and are placing an order for what you want.

List things just as you would when ordering a meal. Order an appetizer, a main meal, some side dishes, and a dessert.

Then begin to feel the anticipation of what is coming. It's the anticipation and the visualizing that help reinforce expectations and strengthen intention.

For example, if your daughter wants a new relationship, her order might sound like this:

"For an appetizer, I'd like a surprisingly delicious good time at a event where I meet my future boyfriend.

"For the main dish, I'd like this person to be intelligent, attractive, and kind and to absolutely adore and appreciate me.

"For the side dish, I'd like him to know how to canoe and want to teach me. For another side, I'd like him to have a good buddy for my friend.

"For dessert, I'd like him to be a good kisser."

VARIATION

If this is done in a group, it might be fun for everyone to write up his or her orders as if they were selections on a menu in a restaurant and then share the menus with each other. They might even want to name their restaurant and take orders. "Anyone want to order something from my Dream Delight Café?"

WHAT'S BEING LEARNED

Teenagers are learning to take a wide-open view of life's possibilities and then focus on the details of their desires. Expecting the order to come helps them stay in a receptive, positive place.

Flip-Flop Stamps

Whether you call them flip-flops or zoris or go-aheads or thongs, these rubber shoes are inexpensive to buy, and if you live near the ocean, you can often find them washed up on the shore. But you don't have to comb beaches to find cheap rubber flip-flops; you might find them lingering and no longer used in the back of the closet.

TYPE OF ATTENTION ENCOURAGED

Focused

MATERIALS

One cleaned flip-flop
Sharp knife or other cutting tool (not to be used by younger children)
Ink pad, sponge with paint, or colored markers
Paper

DIRECTIONS

Draw a simple design on the flip-flop. Then carefully cut the design out.

If you don't have an ink pad, pour some tempera paint into a sponge for a pad. Press the rubber into the sponge first and then onto a piece of paper.

VARIATION

Use a marking pen to cover the design, then press it on the paper.

WHAT'S BEING LEARNED

Teenagers must certainly focus in this activity in order to carefully cut out the design without messing it up or hurting themselves. The opportunity to make a unique and personal stamp all their own should also hold their attention.

Word Puzzles

Children who are diagnosed with ADD are thought to be strongly visual thinkers. Because of this, they are often able to look at a group of letters and rearrange them to make another word, such as in an anagram game. In this game, all children are challenged to make words out of a group of selected letters. The letters can be presented backwards or mixed up. Adjust the challenge to fit the teen's skill level through your presentation and your choice of word.

TYPE OF ATTENTION ENCOURAGED

Open

MATERIALS

Index cards
Pen

DIRECTIONS

Write each letter of the alphabet on a separate index card. Make more than one card for each vowel and common consonants.

There are three ways to play:

1. Backwards. Lay out the cards so that a word is written backwards. Without touching the cards, your player has to guess what the word would spell when written forward. After he guesses, he can rearrange the letters to see if he is right.

2. Jumbled. Choose any word you want and lay out the letters of that word in no particular order. The player's job is to look at all those letters and rearrange them in his head to form a word. After he does, he can rearrange the letters on the cards.

3. List. Give your teens a list of words or let them come up with a list. Then have them either spell out a word backwards or jumble it and

challenge each other to solve the word puzzle and see how many they can figure out.

These same games can be played with younger children or a mixed age group by giving the players words that suit their skill level.

VARIATIONS

♦ Give children clues, especially if they seem to be stuck. For example, a clue to the letters "wetasre" could be "It's something useful to have if you get cold."

♦ Use toilet paper rolls instead of index cards. Write a letter on each roll and stand it on end. One advantage to rolls is that they stand up nicely and can be knocked down like bowling pins at the end of each game, which gives an added zest to the activity. The other advantage is that it gives us a chance to reuse those nice pieces of rolled cardboard.

WHAT'S BEING LEARNED

Children are learning to open up to word possibilities by visualizing or physically trying out various combinations until they find the right one or ones.

This is an especially useful way to help children maintain their attention when studying for a spelling test. If they can recognize the word backwards and jumbled, they can easily spell it forwards!

Index ~

A

Accentuate the Positive (teen game), 145

Achy Breaky Heart (teen game), 146–147

ADD (Attention Deficit Disorder), 2, 173

Adolescents. *See* Teens

All the Things You Can Think Of (6- to 12-year-olds), 111–112

Annoyed with the Flower Bud (teen game), 147–149

Another Viewpoint (3- to 6-year olds), 74–75

Armstrong, T., 2

Art de Deux (3- to 6-year-olds), 76–77

Art games: Art de Deux (3- to 6-year-olds), 76–77; Flip-Flop Stamps (teens), 172; Junk Box Art (6- to 12-year-olds), 120–121; My Special Things (teen game), 152–153; Paint the World, 99–100; Paper Plethora (6- to 12-year-olds), 132–133; Potato Puppets (6- to 12-year-olds), 133–135; Self-Portraits (teens), 166–167; Sensory Matching (6- to 12-year-olds), 135–137; Shelf Paper Story (6- to 12-year-olds), 126–127; Tile Painting (6- to 12-year-olds), 137–138; Toothpick Art (6- to 12-year-olds), 141–142

Attention: challenge of capturing children's, 1–4; focused type of, 1; open and global form of, 1; shifting from open to focused, 2; *See also specific focused and open attention games by age*

Author contact information, 5

B

Back Writing (6- to 12-year-olds), 112–113

Backwards Time Management (6- to 12-year-olds), 138–140

Ball playing (toddler game), 60–61

Bat the Ball (infant game), 31–32

Batting Practice (3- to 6-year olds), 77–78

Being a Radio (toddler game), 59–60

Bracelet of Leaves (toddler game), 47

C

Can You Hear What I Hear? (infant game), 24–25

Catch a Falling Scarf (toddler game), 60–61

Cautions: keeping objects out of children's mouths, 53; never leave child alone near shallow water, 48

Children: ADD (Attention Deficit Disorder) and, 2, 173; challenge of capturing attention of, 1–4; toddlers (1- to 3-year-olds), 45–70. *See also* Infants; Teen games

Children (3- to 6-year-olds): general information on, 71; time outs for, 85–86

Children's games (3- to 6-year-olds): Another Viewpoint, 74–75; Art de Deux, 76–77; Deck of Cards, 88–89; Expanding Interest, 114–116; Going on a Monster Hunt, 97–99; Hand on Top, 89–90; The Happening Book, 78–80; How Many?, 90–91; Indoor Picture Hunt, 91–92; Lessons from the Rocks, 80–81; Mexican Yo-Yo, 92–93; Mini-Montessori, 94–97; Mismatched Tea Party, 81–83; My Story Is the Best Story, 73–74; Paint the World, 99–100; The Perfect Gifts, 100–103; Plenty Peanut Hunt, 84–85; Regroup Time, 85–86; Shadow Games, 87; Word Matching, 105–107

Children's games (6- to 12-year-olds): All the Things You Can Think Of, 111–112; Back Writing, 112–113; Backwards Time Management, 138–140; Belly Counts, 113–114; Expanding Interest, 114–116; Focused Fidgeting, 116–117; general information on, 109; Guess How Old, 117–118; How Do You Look?, 119–120; I'm the Teacher, 129–130; Junk Box Art, 120–121; My Mind Is a TV Screen, 130–132; Name the Sounds, 121–122; Navigator, 122–123; Paper Plethora, 132–133; Police Report, 123–124; Potato Puppets, 133–135; Ring of String, 125–126; Sensory Matching, 135–137; Shelf Paper Story, 126–127; Thinking Box, 127–129; Tile Painting, 137–138; Toe Stepping, 140–141; Toothpick Art, 141–142

Creativity. *See* Art games

Curiosity (infant), 35–36, 39

D

Dangling Toys (infant game), 28–31

Deck of Cards (3- to 6-year-olds), 88–89

E

The Enchantment of Water (toddler game), 48–49

Exercise games: Back Writing (6- to 12-year-olds), 112–113; First Exercises (infants), 17–20

Expanding Interest (3- to 6-year-olds), 114–116

Eye-hand coordination: Bat the Ball (infants), 31–32; Batting Practice (3- to 6-year olds), 77–78; Catch a Falling Scarf (toddlers), 60–61

F

The Feely Game (toddler game), 54–55

First Exercises (infant game), 17–20

Five Good Moments (teen game), 149–150

Flip-Flop Stamps (teen game), 172

Focused attention: described, 1; shifting from global to, 2

Focused attention games (3- to 6-year-olds): Another Viewpoint, 74–75; Art de Deux, 76–77; Batting Practice, 77–78; Deck of Cards, 88–89; Expanding Interest, 114–116; Focused Fidgeting, 116–117; Guess How Old, 117–118; Hand on Top, 89–90; The Happening Book, 78–80; How Many?, 90–91; Indoor Picture Hunt, 91–92; Lessons from the Rocks, 80–81; Mexican Yo-Yo, 92–93; Mini-Montessori, 94–97; Mismatched Tea Party, 81–83; My Story Is the Best Story, 73–74; Paint the World, 99–100; The Perfect Gifts, 100–103; Plenty Peanut Hunt, 84–85; Regroup Time, 85–86; Shadow Games, 87; Sounds Right, 104–105; Word Matching, 105–107

Focused attention games (6- to 12-year-olds): Back Writing, 112–113; Backwards Time Management, 138–140; Belly Counts, 113–114; I'm the Teacher, 129–130; Junk Box Art, 120–121; Navigator, 122–123; Paper Plethora, 132–133; Police Report, 123–124; Potato Puppets, 133–135; Ring of String, 125–126; Sensory Matching, 135–137; Shelf Paper Story, 126–127; Thinking Box, 127–129; Tile Painting, 137–138; Toe Stepping, 140–141; Toothpick Art, 141–142

Focused attention games (infants): Bat the Ball, 31–32; Being a Radio, 59–60; Can You Hear What I Hear?, 24–25; Dangling Toys, 28–31; First Exercises, 17–20; Follow My Face, 9–11; The Glory of Hands, 13–14; High Chair Fling, 32–34; Ice Cube on a Tray, 34–35; If It Doesn't Hurt—It's a Toy, 35–37; A Light Touch, 22–24; Perfect Rattles, 15–17; Pokey Pudding Hole, 27–28; Sock on a Bottle, 14–15; A Spotlight in the Dark, 37–39; Stick Out Your Tongue, 11–12; Where'd It Go?, 41–43

Focused attention games (teens): Achy Breaky Heart, 146–147; Annoyed with the Flower Bud, 147–149; Five Good Moments, 149–150; Flip-Flop Stamps, 172; Getting the Priorities, 150–152; The Home Videographer, 169–170; I'm Like That Sometimes, 153–154; Imagine That!, 155–156; Life Is a Movie, and You Are the Star!, 158–159; My Special Things, 152–153; Name the Consequences, 162–164; Postcard Diaries, 164–165; Scriptwriter, 165–166; Self-Portraits, 166–167; Send Joy to Bulgaria, 156–158; Ten Breaths, 167–169; Waiter, Take My Order, 170–171

Focused attention games (toddlers): Bracelet of Leaves, 47; Catch a Falling Scarf, 60–61; The Enchantment of Water, 48–49; The Feely Game, 54–55; Follow the Floating Feather, 49–50; From Beginning to End, 57–58; Instant Picture, 61–62; Kaleidoscope, 63–64; The Knocking Game, 50–51; Magnet Hunt, 64–66; Ooh—Smell This!, 67–69; Ping-Pong Balls and Coffee Cans, 51–52; Put a Lid on It, 66–67; What Is That Sound?, 55–57; What's in the Sock?, 69–70; You've Got Mail, 62–63

Focused Fidgeting (3- to 6-year-olds), 116–117

Follow the Floating Feather (toddler game), 49–50

Follow My Face (infant game), 9–11

Frère Jacques (song), 18

From Beginning to End (toddler game), 57–58

G

Getting the Priorities (teen game), 150–152

Gift giving (3- to 6-year-olds), 100–103

The Glory of Hands (infant game), 13–14

Going on a Monster Hunt (3- to 6-year-olds), 97–99

Guess How Old (3- to 6-year-olds), 117–118

H

Hand on Top (3- to 6-year-olds), 89–90

The Happening Book (3- to 6-year-olds), 78–80

Hearing games: Can You Hear What I Hear? (infants), 24–25; The Knocking Game (1- to 3-year-olds), 50–51; Name the Sounds (6- to 12-year-olds), 121–122; Sounds Right (3- to 6-year-olds), 104–105; What Is That Sound? (1- to 3-year-olds), 55–57

High Chair Fling (infant game), 32–34

High-and-seek games: Surprise Me (toddlers), 53–54; Where'd It Go? (infants), 41–43

The Home Videographer (teen game), 169–170

How Do You Look? (3- to 6-year-olds), 119–120

How Many? (3- to 6-year-olds), 90–91

How to Reach and Teach ADD/ADHD Children (Rief), 4

I

Ice Cube on a Tray (infant game), 34–35

If It Doesn't Hurt—It's a Toy (infant game), 35–37

I'm Like That Sometimes (teen game), 153–154

I'm the Teacher (6- to 12-year-olds), 129–130

Imagine That! (teen game), 155–156

Indoor Picture Hunt (3- to 6-year-olds), 91–92

Infant games: Bat the Ball, 31–32; Can You Hear What I Hear?, 24–25; Dangling Toys, 28–31; First Exercises, 17–20; Follow My Face, 9–11; general information related to, 7–8; The Glory of Hands, 13–14; High Chair Fling, 32–34; Ice Cube on a Tray, 34–35; If It Doesn't Hurt—It's a Toy, 35–37; A Light Touch, 22–24; Perfect Rattles, 15–17; Pokey Pudding Hole, 27–28; Sock on a Bottle, 14–15; A Spotlight in the Dark, 37–39; Stick Out Your Tongue, 11–12; A Very Merry Unbirthday, 26–27; Visually Amused, 21–22; What's Out There?, 39–41; Where'd It Go?, 41–43

Infants: general information on games for, 7–8; love of high-and-seek by, 41; love of throwing by, 32–33; natural curiosity of, 35–36, 39; touching activity by, 28–29; touching as feedback to, 22. *See also* Children

Instant Picture (toddler game), 61–62

J

Junk Box Art (6- to 12-year-olds), 120–121

K

Kaleidoscope (toddler game), 63–64

The Knocking Game (toddler game), 50–51

L

Language games: Back Writing (6- to 12-year-olds), 112–113; How Do You Look? (nonverbal language), 119–120; I'm the Teacher (6- to 12-year-olds), 129–130; My Story Is the Best Story (3- to 6-year-olds), 73–74; Shelf Paper Story (6- to 12-year-olds), 126–127; Word Matching (3- to 6-year-olds), 105–107. *See also* Reading games; Writing games

Lessons from the Rocks (3- to 6-year-olds), 80–81

Levine, M., 2

Life Is a Movie, and You Are the Star! (teen game), 158–159

A Light Touch (infant game), 22–24

List Your Options (teen game), 160–162

M

Magnet Hunt (toddler game), 64–66

Mexican Yo-Yo (3- to 6-year-olds), 92–93

A Mind at a Time (Levine), 2

Mini-Montessori (3- to 6-year-olds), 94–97

Mismatched Tea Party (3- to 6-year-olds), 81–83

Mr. Roger's Neighborhood (TV show), 39

My Mind Is a TV Screen (6- to 12-year-olds), 130–132

My Special Things (teen game), 152–153

My Story Is the Best Story (3- to 6-year-olds), 73–74

Myth of the ADD Child (Armstrong), 2

N

Name the Consequences (teen game), 162–164

Name the Sounds (6- to 12-year-olds), 121–122

Navigator (6- to 12-year-olds), 122–123

O

Ooh—Smell This! (toddler game), 67–69

Open attention games (3- to 6-year-olds): Another Viewpoint, 74–75; Art de Deux, 76–77; Expanding Interest, 114–116; Focused Fidgeting, 116–117; Going on a Monster Hunt, 97–99; Guess How Old, 117–118; The Happening Book, 78–80; How Do You Look?, 119–120; Indoor Picture Hunt, 91–92; Mismatched Tea Party, 81–83; My Story Is the Best Story, 73–74; Paint the World, 99–100; The Perfect Gifts, 100–103

Open attention games (6- to 12-year-olds): All the Things You Can Think Of, 111–112; Junk Box Art, 120–121; My Mind Is a TV Screen, 130–132; Name the Sounds, 121–122; Navigator, 122–123; Paper Plethora, 132–133; Police Report, 123–124; Sensory Matching, 135–137; Shelf Paper Story, 126–127

Open attention games (infants): Can You Hear What I Hear?, 24–25; Dangling Toys, 28–31; If It Doesn't Hurt—It's a Toy, 35–37; A Spotlight in the Dark, 37–39; A Very Merry Unbirthday, 26–27; Visually Amused, 21–22; What's Out There?, 39–41; Where'd It Go?, 41–43

Open attention games (teens): Achy Breaky Heart, 146–147; Five Good Moments, 149–150; Getting the Priorities, 150–152; The Home Videographer, 169–170; Imagine That!, 155–156; Life Is a Movie, and You Are the Star!, 158–159; List Your Options, 160–162; My Special Things, 152–153; Name the Consequences, 162–164; Postcard Diaries, 164–165; Ten Breaths, 167–169; Waiter, Take My Order, 170–171; Word Puzzles, 173–174

Open attention games (toddlers): Being a Radio, 59–60; Bracelet of Leaves, 47; Catch a Falling Scarf, 60–61; The Feely Game, 54–55; The Knocking Game, 50–51; Magnet Hunt, 64–66; Ooh—Smell This!, 67–69; Surprise Me, 53–54; What Is That Sound?, 55–57

P

Paint the World (3- to 6-year-olds), 99–100

Paper Plethora (6- to 12-year-olds), 132–133

The Perfect Gifts (3- to 6-year-olds), 100–103

Perfect Rattles (infant game), 15–17

Ping-Pong Balls and Coffee Cans (toddler game), 51–52

Plenty Peanut Hunt (3- to 6-year-olds), 84–85

Pokey Pudding Hole (infant game), 27–28

Police Report (6- to 12-year-olds), 123–124

Postcard Diaries (teen game), 164–165

Potato Puppets (6- to 12-year-olds), 133–135

Put a Lid on It (toddler game), 66–67

R

Reading games: I'm the Teacher (6- to 12-year-olds), 129–130; My Mind Is a TV Screen (6- to 12-year-olds), 130–132; Sensory Matching (6- to 12-year-olds), 135–137; Word Matching (3- to 6-year-olds), 105–107; Word Puzzles (teens), 173–174. *See also* Language games; Writing games

Regroup Time (3- to 6-year-olds), 85–86

Rief, S., 4

Ring of String (6- to 12-year-olds), 125–126

S

Scriptwriter (teen game), 165–166

Self-Portraits (teen game), 166–167

Send Joy to Bulgaria (teen game), 156–158

Sensory Matching (6- to 12-year-olds), 135–137

Shadow Games (3- to 6-year-olds), 87

Shelf Paper Story (6- to 12-year-olds), 126–127

Sher, B., 5

Smelling game (toddler game), 66–67

Sock on a Bottle (infant game), 14–15

Sound games: Can You Hear What I Hear? (infants), 24–25; The Knocking Game (1- to 3-year-olds), 50–51; Name the Sounds (6- to 12-year-olds), 121–122; Sounds Right (3- to 6-year-olds), 104–105; What Is That Sound? (1- to 3-year-olds), 55–57

Sounds Right (3- to 6-year-olds), 104–105

A Spotlight in the Dark (infant game), 37–39

Stick Out Your Tongue (infant game), 11–12

Surprise Me (toddler game), 53–54

T

Teen games: Accentuate the Positive, 145; Achy Breaky Heart, 146–147; Annoyed with the Flower Bud, 147–149; Five Good Moments, 149–150; Flip-Flop Stamps, 172; general information about, 143; Getting the Priorities, 150–152; The Home Videographer, 169–170; I'm Like That Sometimes, 153–154; Imagine That!, 155–156; Life Is a Movie, and You Are the Star!, 158–159; List Your Options, 160–162; My Special Things, 152–153; Name the Consequences, 162–164; Postcard Diaries, 164–165; Scriptwriter, 165–166; Self-Portraits, 166–167; Send Joy to Bulgaria, 156–158; Ten Breaths, 167–169; Waiter, Take My Order, 170–171. *See also* Children

Ten Breaths (teen game), 167–169

Thinking Box (6- to 12-year-olds), 127–129

Throwing games: Catch a Falling Scarf (toddlers), 60–61; High Chair Fling (infants), 32–34

Tile Painting (6- to 12-year-olds), 137–138

Time management game, 138–140

Time outs activity (Regroup Time), 85–86

Toddler games (1- to 3-year-olds): Being a Radio, 59–60; Bracelet of Leaves, 47; Catch a Falling Scarf, 60–61; The Enchantment of Water, 48–49; The Feely Game, 54–55; Follow the Floating Feather, 49–50; From Beginning to End, 57–58; Kaleidoscope, 63–64; The Knocking Game, 50–51; Magnet Hunt, 64–66; Ooh—Smell This!, 67–69; Ping-Pong Balls and Coffee Cans, 51–52; Put a Lid on It, 66–67; Surprise Me, 53–54; What Is That Sound?, 55–57; What's in the Sock?, 69–70; You've Got Mail, 62–63

Toddlers (1- to 3-year-olds): gathering information through touch by, 54; general information on games for, 45; identification of sounds by, 50, 55; Instant Picture, 61–62; keeping objects out of mouth caution for, 53; shallow water caution for, 48

Toe Stepping (6- to 12-year-olds), 140–141

Toothpick Art (6- to 12-year-olds), 141–142

Touching: infants and, 22, 28–29; toddlers and, 54

Traveling games: All the Things You Can Think Of (6- to 12-year-olds), 111–112; Being a Radio (toddlers), 59–60; How Many? (3- to 6-year-olds), 90–91; Instant Picture (toddlers), 61–62; Navigator (6- to 12-year-olds), 122–123; Postcard Diaries (teens), 164–165

V

A Very Merry Unbirthday (infant game), 26–27

Visualization games: Imagine That! (teens), 155–156; My Mind Is a TV Screen (6- to 12-year-olds), 130–132; Word Puzzles (teens), 173–174

Visually Amused (infant game), 21–22

W

Waiter, Take My Order (teen game), 170–171

Wellness model, 2–3

What Is That Sound? (toddler game), 55–57

What's Out There? (infant game), 39–41

What's in the Sock? (toddler game), 69–70

Where'd It Go? (infant game), 41–43

Word Matching (3- to 6-year-olds), 105–107

Word Puzzles (teens), 173–174

Writing games: Scriptwriter (teens), 165–166; Word Matching (3- to 6-year-olds), 105–107; Word Puzzles (teens), 173–174. *See also* Language games; Reading games

Y

You've Got Mail (toddler game), 62–63